Choose Happy

Choose Happy

Easy Strategies
TO FIND YOUR BLISS

Sarah Gregg

ROCK POINT
QUARTOKNOWS.COM
NEW YORK, NY

© 2021 Quarto Publishing Group USA Inc.

First published in 2021 by Rock Point,
an imprint of The Quarto Group
142 West 36th Street, 4th Floor
New York, NY 10018, USA
T (212) 779-4972 F (212) 779-6058
www.QuartoKnows.com

Rock Point titles are also available at discount for retail, wholesale, promotional, and bulk purchase. For details, contact the Special Sales Manager by email at specialsales@quarto.com or by mail at The Quarto Group, Attn: Special Sales Manager, 100 Cummings Center Suite 265D, Beverly, MA 01915, USA.

Library of Congress Cataloging-in-Publication Data

Names: Gregg, Sarah, author.
Title: Choose happy: easy strategies to find your bliss/ Sarah Gregg.
Description: New York, NY : Rock Point, 2021. | Series: Live well |
   Includes bibliographical references. | Summary: "Sarah Gregg,
   neurolinguistic programming practitioner and author of Find Your Flow
   (Rock Point, 2020), uses the practices of positive psychology to gently
   guide the reader through healing their past, enjoying the present, and
   fulfilling their future to improve their well-being for a life full of
   joy, contentedness, and hope. With Choose Happy, happiness will be
   elusive no longer. Includes reflections and quick daily exercises, all
   wrapped up in an attractive, fun, and inspiring package"-- Provided by
   publisher.
Identifiers: LCCN 2020043177 (print) | LCCN 2020043178 (ebook) | ISBN
   9781631067129 (hardcover) | ISBN 9780760368121 (ebook)
Subjects: LCSH: Happiness. | Emotions. | Self-realization.
Classification: LCC BF575.H27 G737 2020 (print) | LCC BF575.H27 (ebook) |
   DDC 158.1--dc23
LC record available at https://lccn.loc.gov/2020043177
LC ebook record available at https://lccn.loc.gov/2020043178

10 9 8 7 6 5 4 3 2 1

ISBN: 978-1-63106-712-9

Publisher: Rage Kindelsperger
Creative Director: Laura Drew
Managing Editor: Cara Donaldson
Project Editor: Leeann Moreau
Cover Design: Laura Drew
Book Design: Shubhani Sarkar, sarkardesignstudio.com

Printed in China

To my husband Chris,
who took the road less traveled with me
and lovingly held my hand with each step.
In every lifetime I'd choose you.

CONTENTS

believe in your future

enjoy your present

happy-ology

"Happiness and freedom begin with
a simple, clear understanding of one principle:
some things are in your control,
and some things are not."

—*Epictetus*

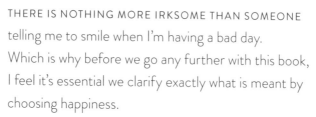

THERE IS NOTHING MORE IRKSOME THAN SOMEONE telling me to smile when I'm having a bad day. Which is why before we go any further with this book, I feel it's essential we clarify exactly what is meant by choosing happiness.

We live in a chaotic, changing world where things can feel outside of our control, including our happiness. Figures point to rising numbers of people feeling anxious and depressed, yet the rhetoric of excessive hope tells us that everyone can have everything they desire if they just put their minds to it. So, why the disconnect? If it's so easy to have it all and be happy, then why are so many of us struggling?

Perhaps it's because our society's insistence that we demonstrate excessive hopefulness has the unintentional consequence of making us feel miserable.

HOW TO BE HAPPY

Firstly, the "just be happy" approach can lead us to reject the painful, sad, and frustrating feelings we have about life. We've learned to view these negative emotions as markers of failure and inadequacy rather than seeing them as what they actually are—a natural and essential part of our humanity.

Indeed, evolutionary psychologists believe there is an upside to feeling down. Negative emotions can act as a clarifying force, jolting us into action. They illuminate areas we need to change and provoke personal realizations. Negative emotions are the cords connecting us to the different versions of our selves waiting on the other side of life's turbulent storms. Although they're deeply unpleasant to feel, it's impossible to completely separate them from our human experience.

Secondly, excessive hopefulness taught us that happiness is equal to having more, and it has instilled the mass mantra, "If I just have x, then I will be happier." We strive for more wealth, success, beauty, status, and praise because we believe when get those things we'll feel happier. But does that work?

Unfortunately not, according to psychologists who have termed this exhausting process the hedonic treadmill. Research has continually shown that enduring happiness doesn't come from a bigger house, job promotion, or even winning the lottery. Of course, we'll feel an initial high, but psychologists contend this soon fades as we adapt to our new normal and gradually return to our baseline level of happiness.[1]

This way of thinking has ballooned our expectations and displaced our everyday hope that small things can make us happy. We shun our ordinary existence and revere extraordinary achievements as a symbol of a life well lived. Sadly, for many of us, it often takes a tragedy to shake us into the sobering realization that happiness was there all along; we just overlooked it. The ordinary was, in fact, extraordinary.

This blink-of-an-eye existence is miraculous, messy, and always in motion. You are a beautiful, unique collection of thirty-seven-trillion cells alive today on planet Earth, floating in space, surrounded by a billion stars. You do not have to hustle or prove your worthiness to be happy.

Happiness is not a reward. It's a consequence of our thoughts, actions, and shifts in perspective.

Choose Happy uses psychology, research, and practical tools to help us choose, not pursue, happiness. And because our minds can wander through time, we'll explore how to choose happy through the lens of your past, future, and present. Now, if your observant brain is screaming "why did she structure the book past, future, present?" I promise, there's good reason. Allow me to explain and set the context for *Choose Happy*.

All moments begin and end in the present. It's where our past is formed, our future is set in motion, and life is experienced.

While this linear narrative of time cleanly fits our physical world, it doesn't reflect the messy mental reality we experience. As my friend once eloquently put, "You are a world within a world." In our minds, the past, present, and future occupy the same space. With a flick of a thought we have the capacity to travel between those three worlds in one moment.

Our ability to mentally time-travel is unique, but it is a superpower we're often ill-equipped to use. When thoughts push open the door to our remembered past and imagined future, consciousness points its arrow inward and we retract from the present moment.

> *Happiness is not a reward. It's a consequence of our thoughts, actions, and shifts in perspective.*

Some journeys into the past and future can boost our happiness as we reminisce over fond memories and dream up an exciting future. However, others can feel uncontrollably hijacked by fear, anger, and rumination, pulling us deeper inward so that we become lost in our thoughts. Like a dense mist, thoughts cloud our minds and life continues, but we're not looking.

We must cultivate the mental discipline to fully engage in the present moment. Otherwise we risk letting those gestures of love slip past unnoticed—leaving jokes at the dinner table unheard and opportunities overlooked.

In *Choose Happy*, you'll learn that no emotion is good or bad, but rather every emotion has its purpose and place. You will understand how to choose which one in your emotional toolkit is best suited for the job and can make you happy.

This book will show you how you can bring happiness back to ordinary, everyday life without losing hope or forgetting how to dream. *Choose Happy* doesn't promise that you'll feel round-the-clock, 24/7 happiness, because it would be unrealistic and damaging to do so. But it does offer resources to help practically guide us towards happier choices, moving us out of the struggle and into happiness. We all deserve to choose happy more empowering choices and to make the most out of our lives. Let this book show you that happiness just on the other side of choice.

SCIENCE *of* BLISS

Often, we try to accumulate what doesn't actually increase our happiness. Research has repeatedly found that while money can buy you some happiness, it's rarely as much as you think. Focusing on increasing our possessions can actually decrease our happiness. In one particular study psychologists found that people who strive to accumulate money, possessions, and status displayed more signs of distress and poor well-being. In contrast, those who focused on personal growth, close relationships, and community experienced more happiness.[2] In short, if you want seven-figure happiness then shift your focus to increasing your experiences, close relationships, and impact on the world—not your possessions.

THE SCIENCE OF HAPPINESS

The science of happiness offers the sound, sturdy, helpful advice we wish we'd been taught at school. It shows us how happiness is possible, with its research informing tools and techniques to build happier lives. And despite its name, happiness isn't the only emotion the researchers are interested in. On the contrary, all emotions—not just the positive ones—are welcome. A study on emotional diversity found that the more emotional diversity we experience, the less likely we are to become depressed and the more likely we are to have healthier habits.[3] Our emotions are rarely the problem. The problem is we think we shouldn't have those emotions, as we fight against how we feel we begin a battle within ourselves.

For me, the importance of understanding the science of happiness runs deeper than an obsession to increase individual moments of joy. Our collective happiness has a long-term impact on the quality of our lives and the contribution we make to the world. Happiness research has found that happier people are healthier, more productive, more helpful, and have better relationships.[4] The happier we are as individuals the greater our capacity to help others feel the same. Every act of happiness towards ourselves and others has meaning for the whole, we are not separate from each other or nature, we are one with all life.

When we each commit to choosing happiness, to living a meaningful life, and believing that we're worthy to receive it, life can respond. The science of happiness doesn't shy away from the truth that it takes work and ownership to carve out a happy life. Happiness is an ongoing, layered journey that continually reveals new territory to explore. You'll need different guides at different stages to navigate your journey, and I hope this book becomes one of them.

happy TIP

Many of us chase happiness without even knowing what it means to us. Take a few minutes to write down your own definition of happiness.

HAPPINESS IS. . .

Happiness is a small word with a big and complex meaning. So, before we journey into how to become happier, let's establish what we mean by happiness.

To keep it succinct, the main points have been distilled into our happy-ology. As a blend of realism and ideology, it aims to communicate what we mean by happiness on an individual and collective level.

- Happiness is the experience of gratitude, contentment, joy, and well-being, as well as the sense that life has meaning and a purpose greater than ourselves.

- Happiness is an acceptance that life can be challenging, painful, and stressful for us all, and the acknowledgment that light exists even in the darkest of times, as "negative" emotions such as anger and sadness can be positive catalysts for growth and change.

- Happiness is not black and white; we experience it in shades. It is possible to feel happy and sad at the same time.

- Happiness is when all the separate parts of life fit together. It's the alignment of our past, present, and future that can give life meaning.

- Happiness is a shared responsibility. Everyone is born worthy of happiness, our job in life on an individual level is to find our own inner happiness, and on a collective level to help others feel happier through our kindness.

- Happiness is a subjective feeling and is personal to each of us.

- Happiness is temporary. We're not going to be one hundred percent happy, one hundred percent of the time, and holding our lives to this unachievable expectation is likely to have the opposite effect.

- Happiness is never underestimating our tremendous ability to surmount what feels insurmountable.

- Happiness is a choice and a journey, not a pursuit or a destination.

EXERCISE

What Makes You Happy?

Happiness leaves its signature feel-good factor trademark on the experiences we have. By asking ourselves what makes us happy we can begin to understand the types of experiences in which happiness appears for us. It's through this understanding of what brings us happiness that we can design our lives around increasing these types of experiences.

This exercise appears very simple but can be quite challenging. Do not be surprised if after writing down just ten things you want to throw your pen across the room. But please stick with it, it's designed to stretch your thinking and spot happiness patterns that occur in your life.

- Find a quiet place to sit and write down a list of thirty things that make you truly, deeply, personally happy.

- After writing your list, review and make a note of the common happiness patterns that appear (e.g. cooking, being with other people, etc).

- Next, on a scale of 1–10 assess how much are you currently incorporating these happiness activities in your everyday life (with one being not at all and ten being my diary is filled with them).

- Pick one thing from your happiness list that you can do today as a sign of your commitment to choosing to be happy.

DECLUTTERING OUR PAST, FUTURE, AND PRESENT

In recent years, we've witnessed a rise in the minimalist movement. A plethora of books and TV shows have flooded our mainstream media, all stressing the negative impact our cluttered homes have on our lives. As a result, people throughout the world have been donating and selling their unwanted possessions, with many selecting their items based on the advice of tidying expert Marie Kondo.

Japanese author Marie Kondo urges us to ask, "Does it spark joy?" when deciding whether an object or article of clothing should remain in our lives. This simple philosophy is easy to grasp and has helped countless people streamline, organize, and feel happier in their homes. But what's this got to do with our inner happiness?

In the same way that our visible external world has become cluttered and overcrowded, so too has our invisible inner world, of which we are the sole inhabitants. Just as we can wander into different rooms in our house, our consciousness can wander into different rooms of our mind, namely our past, future, and present. And if we've been sweeping our problems under the rug or fighting them with fear, then it's no wonder that so many of us feel overwhelmed dwelling in our internal chaos.

While our mind's time-traveling ability plays a vital role in helping us plan, learn, and grow, it can disrupt our happiness without careful management. Irrespective of individual circumstances, anyone's mind can cause them to feel the pain of the remembered past or fear the imagined future. That's why when we explore choosing happiness, we'll do it in the context of the past, future, and present.

A happy mind is one in which we can wander into our past, shuffle through its memories—good and bad—and learn from them. We can glide into our present, feeling content to just be in the moment as we allow ourselves to feel the joy of existing. And we can open the door to the future with hope, blissfully daydreaming about what's yet to come. When our past, present, and future seamlessly interconnect, thoughts can flow freely, we feel aligned, and we trust we're where we're meant to be.

But let's take a moment to clarify our expectations, as my intention isn't to add to any existing pressure to try to have a perfectly tidy mind and home. I'm in no way suggesting your mind should be a spotless haven for positive thoughts with every negative thought tossed out. Our minds are more likely to be a beautiful mess than they are a minimalist's dream. And negative emotions can spark spectacular changes. There is beauty in sitting in discomfort, seeing the light and shadows it brings, and how it creates new ways of thinking. When it comes to happiness, imperfection is really perfect when you learn to love your surroundings.

Just as Marie Kondo asks the "Does it spark joy?" when it comes to tidying our homes. We can use the question "Will it bring me happiness?" when sorting through our inner world. This question can help us choose thoughts, actions, and beliefs that are helpful to our long-term happiness. And when it comes to saying goodbye to the thoughts that no longer serve

happy TIP Happiness and pleasure are different, so when considering "Will it bring me happiness?" think about the long-term impact of your choices as opposed to the short-term gain. Yes, an extra glass of wine or avoiding a difficult conversation might bring immediate pleasure, but in the long run they may not bring happiness.

us, we can do so with compassion. We can thank comfort eating for wanting to make us feel better, tell fear we appreciate its concern and advise anger that we've heard how much that person hurt us.

We can do all this while firmly letting these thoughts know that their strategies are now causing us harm, so it's time to make a different, more helpful choice. Perhaps we'll even donate their learning to others who are facing a similar situation. But above all else, as we each consider the question "Will it bring me happiness?" we'll need to embrace and feel at ease with its subjectivity. If we are to grow in our understanding of what happiness is to us, we'll need to get used to happiness not being black and white, or what other people do or don't have.

Happiness is a feeling more than a thing.

RECOGNIZING THE CHOICE GAP

We make our choices in a challenging, fast-paced world. And choices for all of us are rarely not as simple as either/or. We each make choices within constraints. We each face our own circumstances, history, and challenges, which means choosing happiness is rarely as cut and dry as saying, "If you just organize your life like this, then you will be happy."

That's why *Choose Happy* draws upon the collective knowledge of science and psychology to inform the content and exercises in the book. While we are all unique, psychology can help us categorize collective human behavior, and we can use its findings to edge us closer to happiness. However, some parts may resonate more than others, so you're encouraged to take what's useful and leave the rest behind.

Our behavior is often a response to the emotional need we are trying to satisfy. Each behavior has a positive intention. For example, people pleasing's intention is to satisfy our need to love and belong. When decluttering your unhelpful responses, pause and ask yourself, "What positive intention does this part of me have?" and "What is a better choice that I can make to satisfy this intention?" to help halt adaptive behaviors.

HOW IT WORKS

Over the following pages, we'll view happiness through the lens of the past, future, and present, focusing on the small changes we can make to edge us closer to happiness.

The overarching intention of *Choose Happy* is to help us make the most of what we have by "thinking little" about the small changes we can make to everyday life.

Each section holds just the right amount of information to plant the seed of change without overwhelming you. **Happy Tips** are quick and easy ways to apply the text of the book. The practical **Exercises** peppered throughout each segment are designed to suggest how you might reach for a happier choice. **Daily Delights** highlight subtle changes you can make to your habits to brighten you outlook. Each **Science of Bliss** section explains a bit of science meant to expand your view of the world. You can dip in and out of this book, just browsing the sections that are most relevant to your life or reading it from cover to cover, the choice is entirely yours.

Finally, because not every aspect of past, future, and present can be covered in this book, a model called the Happiness Ladder has been developed for choosing happiness in difficult times. You can use this model any time to help move you forward toward a happier choice.

EXERCISE

Establish Your Happiness Connection

This is a technique based on neuro-linguistic programming and is designed to establish your happiness connection. It will help you understand what happiness feels like in your body and to tap into the sensations that this emotion elicits for you. For some people, happiness feels like it moves around in their stomach, for others it rests still near their heart. Try it and notice what happiness feels like for you.

- Close your eyes and think of a happy memory. Notice who you are with and what you are doing. As you picture the scene playing like a movie in your mind, turn the volume up and make the colors brighter.

- Next, when the scene is really vivid, notice where happiness lives in your body. Where is that feeling located? Can you place your hand over the location? Does it move up or down? If you could picture this feeling of happiness with color, what would it be?

- As you open your eyes, make a note of your experience or draw a picture/symbol of what you feel happiness looks like to you.

The more you can tap into this feeling, the more we can recognize and open ourselves up to happiness. It's important to remember if you struggled to access this memory or found unwanted thoughts drifting in, perhaps again tomorrow. Or look through old photographs of happier times to help prompt those feelings. Remember, it's normal and natural to struggle to connect with our inner happiness if we haven't accessed it in a while.

THE HAPPINESS LADDER

While it's necessary to recognize the complexities that surround happiness at an individual and global level, we'd be overwhelmed (and this book would never end) if we attempted to explore everything. As this book can't cover every scenario but wants to add the best value, I've developed a model called the Happiness Ladder that can be applied to almost any situation in everyday life.

In *Choose Happy*, we imagine happiness as a ladder, with the bottom rung being the low emotional state you feel, and the top rung being the higher (more positive) emotional state in which you wish to respond. The aim is to move up the ladder through a **recognize, reach**, and **respond** approach. This approach has been adapted from elements of neuro-linguistic programming, mindfulness, and other therapies to help you choose happiness.

happy **TIP** You can use these journal prompts to help you communicate with your feelings. Grab a pen and paper and answer the following questions: What emotion am I feeling right now? What's this emotion trying to tell me? What's the positive intention of my emotion (e.g. to keep you safe from harm)?

Often when we feel sadness, fear, or anxiety, our strategy is to fight, resist, or evade these feelings. We can view them as unnatural, unwanted, and a sign that we are failing or broken. These thoughts can cause us to overreact or downplay our emotions, neither of which are particularly helpful in the long run. But before we can reach for a more useful response, we first need to recognize and accept how we feel.

At the recognize stage of the ladder, you'll allow yourself just to feel what you feel without judgment. Simply sit with or invite in your emotions, viewing them neither as an enemy or a friend. It's through recognizing and accepting how we feel that we can move from "I feel so sad that I am sad" to simply "I feel sad." This helps us separate and distance ourselves from the inner struggle and approach it with greater objectivity.

The overall goal at the recognize stage is to be kinder and less judgmental about how we feel. This enables us to gain a sense of perspective so we can make a better decision about how to move forward.

While this may sound strange, I would encourage you to also thank the emotion for showing up. Just take a moment to recognize its positive intention, appreciate it for showing up, and then let your mind know it's time to reach for a more helpful way of thinking.

happy TIP | If your choice doesn't seem to be having the desired impact, consider whether circumstances have changed or if your choice has brought light to a bigger issue. If it has, it's a good idea to climb back down the ladder and start the process again.

In this stage, we move from knowing our emotions to managing them. Reach is based on the hope that even in our most challenging times, we can reach for a response that can ease our suffering. At this stage, the goal is to edge ourselves closer to happiness. It begins with merely exploring "what if I do" or "what if I don't" scenarios as we harness our mind's unique ability to play out future scenarios.

Consider the following questions to help guide your thoughts:

- What if I do choose a different way to view this situation? What is more helpful to believe? How does that shape my behavior? Does that choice move me closer or further away from how I want to feel?

- What if I don't adjust the way I think and feel about this situation? How does that shape my behavior? Does that move me closer or further away from how I want to feel?

Daily Delights

Happiness can sometimes feel like it's always just over the horizon. It's waiting for us in the next big thing. We're so busy optimizing time, amplifying our abilities, and hacking our brains to get there faster, we overlook the small stuff.

Let's be honest, the small stuff is not sexy. It is the commonsense stuff that's rarely common practice in our lives. But the marginal gains that can be made by improving the micro-moments in our lives can amount to significant improvements in our happiness levels.

RESPOND WITH ACTION, OPENNESS, AND CURIOSITY

Respond is the top rung of our ladder, and as the name suggests, it centers on taking action because good intentions are rarely enough. The respond stage of the process requires openness and curiosity to see what works. We're aiming to simply test out if this new way of thinking can move us toward happiness or not.

What is the first small action you can take as evidence of change in your response? Consider what small steps you could take each day to align your actions and emotions with your desired response. Be kind to yourself during this process and show yourself compassion. It's normal that our choices may have to change as our circumstances unfold.

We may not always be in control of our external circumstances, but we are always in control of how we choose to respond to them. The more we cultivate and flex our choice muscle, the more we become aware that choice is our key out of feeling trapped by our failures, upsets, and setbacks. Life responds to our choices, we act and it responds. The Happiness Ladder provides a framework to pause, slow down, and shift from reacting to responding with intention. When everything feels chaotic, overwhelming, and out of control, choice offers a happy place we can retreat to.

Choose Happy.
Choose to see its flickering
light in this moment and the
next. These moments are your
life. Your future is shaped by
how you'll use the present.
And the present is experienced
by how much you're willing to
release yourself from the past.
To choose happy is to create a
bond with life, to enter into
a blissful union that says
I'm here, I'm worthy, I matter,
my life has meaning.

learn
FROM YOUR
past

"The secret of change is to focus
all your energy not fighting the old,
but on building the new."

—**Socrates**

OUR PAST CAN BE AKIN TO AN UNWANTED HOUSE guest. We can't wait for them to leave, only to find, years later, that we're still cleaning up their mess. Our pasts may be unique, but unwanted memories pester us all. We're unable to alter what happened, but we can change the impact it has on the present and future.

However, changing our perception of the past doesn't mean we need to rip out our roots and forget who we are and what we've experienced. Instead, the strategy adopted here is to identify the dead branches of our past and saw them off so we can grow.

THE HABIT ADVANTAGE

"A nail is driven out by another nail;
habit is overcome by habit."

—*Erasmus*

Our past behavior can be relived in the present through our habits. Habits are automatic behaviors that we execute without even thinking, whether it's checking our phone first thing in the morning or putting our shoes on before we leave the house. Habits are ingrained over time and account for forty percent of our daily activities.[5]

While some habits may enhance happiness, others can create a cycle of unhappiness that we struggle to break. Perhaps it's secretly eating to relieve sadness or staying up too late to watch TV to reclaim time.

Regardless of our individual vice, these small unhelpful habits share the ability to elicit momentary pleasure followed by feelings of regret, shame, and general unhappiness.

Part of letting go of the past involves dissolving past habits that no longer serve us. This change doesn't require an overhaul of our lives, in fact, just a bit of tweaking here and there can have a significant impact.

Habits remove the effort of choice from life because we perform them without thinking. For instance, we rarely sit on the sofa debating if we should put our shoes on before we leave the house. We just automatically do it.

Our habits enable our brain to conserve energy so we can focus on what matters most, and what's more, because good and bad habits are formed in the same way, we can use them to work for us and not against us. To do this, we need to understand the science of how habits are formed.

Habits have a three-part formula: cue, behavior, and reward. Think about when you brush your teeth at night as an example. Your cue is bedtime, the behavior is brushing your teeth, and the reward is a clean feeling. By understanding this formula, research has shown we can work with it to shift our focus toward automatic habits that make us happy at any age.

Be patient, changing a habit takes time. Studies suggest it can take anywhere between 18 and 254 days to form a new habit.[6] The key to change is repetition: the more you repeat the desired new behavior, the more your neurons will fire and rewire to replace the old pattern of behavior. Over time, your desired behavior will become a habit, making it more effortless and automatic.

SCIENCE *of* BLISS

As James Clear notes in his book, *Atomic Habits,* "The difference a tiny improvement can make over time is astounding. Here's how the math works out: if you can get one percent better each day for one year, you'll end up thirty-seven times better by the time you're done."[7]

HABITS AND HAPPINESS

Our ability to change our past habits and develop healthier and happier habits can have an enormous impact on our well-being. As our desired behaviors—like going for a run after work or meditating in the morning—become automatic, happiness flows with greater ease. And while this all sounds simple, the reality is that creating and breaking habits can be something we struggle to do. But research has shown a few simple strategies that can help us.

Firstly, it's essential to start small, as research shows small changes are more effective to our daily routine than elaborate changes.[8]

Secondly, consider how you could habit stack. Habit stacking involves using existing habits to create more positive ones. For instance, I drink coffee first thing in the morning and use this time to do my journal routine. Other examples might include walking on the treadmill while watching your favorite show or doing some push-ups while running a bath.

Thirdly, pay attention to your environmental cues. Research demonstrates that environmental cues are the triggers for our habits. Therefore, it's crucial to set up the right environment for yourself.[9] So that might be putting the gym bag at the front door or replacing the wine in the fridge with a soft drink. These cues make it easier to interrupt your pattern loops and build new ones.

EXERCISE

Change Your Past Habits

Changing unhelpful habits we've accumulated in the past requires aware-ness and repetition. Here is a useful exercise to start the process of choosing happier habits.

- Write down the habit you want to create or change (be specific and start small).

- Write down the cue that will prompt the behavior (e.g. it's lunchtime so it's time to go for a walk).

- Write down the reward you will give yourself (e.g. listening to your favorite music or podcast).

Challenge yourself to complete your new habit every day for the next seven days.

LETTING GO
OF PAST ANGER

"Anybody can become angry—that is easy,
but to be angry with the right person and
to the right degree and at the right time
and for the right purpose, and in the right way—
that is not within everybody's power and is not easy."

—*Aristotle*

nger from the past can be an unwelcome travel companion on our journey through life. Silently lingering by our side, anger waits for its trigger to spark an emotional inferno in our present. I'm certainly no stranger to hauling anger from the past into my present. Indeed, I've felt anger so strong that just the simple mention of a person's name has been enough to flick a switch.

Anger can set our hearts racing and cloud our judgment, sending angry words spewing from our mouths. Memories of our perceived mistreatment seem to flood back like it happened yesterday. And often, once our anger has been released, regret over how we've responded follows.

In those moments of fury, we can feel almost powerless to stop it. It's like an angry gremlin of the past has hijacked our level-headed brain and taken up an unwelcome residence in our minds. But what exactly is happening in your brain when you get angry? And how do you let go of anger from the past?

ANGER IS A UNIVERSAL EMOTION

Firstly, we should recognize that feeling angry doesn't automatically categorize you as a bad person. Anger is a common and natural human emotion that our brains are hardwired to experience. Indeed, sometimes outrage isn't destructive and can create positive change in politics and readdressing inequality. Anger is a primitive feeling also experienced by animals, occurring when a perceived threat to you or another person is detected.[10]

While anger is natural, left unchecked, it can destroy relationships and careers, and leave you with feelings of sincere regret. And although we each have our specific triggers, people typically feel angry when events unfold unexpectedly or people respond in ways that don't match our expectations of how they ought to behave. As Hannah Devlin, the *Guardian*'s science correspondent writes, "We are constantly— often subconsciously—weighing up what we expect to happen in any situation..." noting that anger occurs "...when there is a mismatch between what we've learned to expect and the hand we're dealt."[11]

> *Anger is a common and natural human emotion that our brains are hardwired to experience.*

ANGER AND HAPPINESS

You don't need to be an expert to grasp that anger can damage our happiness, but don't get angry at yourself with being angry. The key to minimizing the harmful impact anger has on us is to understand and work with this natural survival response.

If you've ever recalled an angry outburst about the past and thought, "I just couldn't seem to help it," you've got a small almond-shaped part of your brain called the amygdala to thank for your lack of perceived control.

The amygdala is part of the old operating mechanism of our brain associated with generating the emotion of anger, and neuroscientists have recently discovered it has ultrafast brain responses. It's this lightning-fast response that causes our reaction to feel automatic or outside of our voluntary control.[12] And if this wasn't enough, once activated, the amygdala cuts off the neural pathways to the rational, logical, and empathic part of your brain—the prefrontal cortex. This reaction causes your attention to narrow as you struggle to see the other person's point of view.[13]

Through understanding this, we can take comfort in two things. Firstly, the narrow-minded, out-of-control angry response is not us. It's just the quick reaction time of our amygdala. And secondly, we have all the resources we need to manage our anger from the past. We just need a better understanding of how to access them.

happy
TIP

Venting doesn't help your anger: According to psychologists, "getting it off your chest" or punching a pillow is not the best way to process anger. Indeed, it can increase feelings of anger, with one study showing that doing nothing at all was more effective at resolving anger than venting.[14]

EXERCISE

Managing Anger for Happiness

If you find yourself getting frustrated, agitated, beeping your horn in traffic, or uncontrollably venting, here are some tips to help bring a sense of calm and manage your anger.

UNDERSTAND YOUR TRIGGERS: Keeping an anger journal of your triggers can help you bring awareness of what triggers your anger (or frustration). Logging your triggers can help you develop effective strategies to increase control of your trigger rather than allow them to control you. Triggers might include feeling criticized, experiencing other people not listening or talking over you, or blaming yourself when you make a mistake.

PRACTICE MINDFULNESS: When you feel triggered, use mindfulness techniques to help get you out of the fight-or-flight instinct of the amygdala and access the rational prefrontal cortex. You can do this by slowing down and mindfully focusing on your breath.

LET GO: Psychotherapists have concluded that "anger is not fully resolved until a conscious decision is made to let go."[15] Today, start the process of letting go of what happened and usher in acceptance that no amount of anger will change or make you feel better about the past.

THE GREAT UNLEARNING

"Every new beginning comes from
some other beginning's end."

—*Seneca*

We come into the world with an essence, a soul, a unique image that's seeking to realize its purpose. The Greeks called this our "daimon," the Romans our "genius," and psychologist James Hillman referred to this as acorn theory. In his work, Hillman contends that we come into this world for a reason, each of us as a bundle of cells that contains a dazzling essence of unique potential. He referred to this essence as an acorn and believed that within us, we each had a calling to be lived. Hillman's work stressed the importance of returning to our essence, allowing our tiny acorns of potential to grow into large oaks.[16]

The problem is our essence of bright and powerful potential is hard to hold and nourish in our young untrained hands. We rely on those around us in our formative years to help develop the skills to nurture our tiny seeds of unique potential. However, adults in our lives often have their ideas of what crafts we should master. And so begins the process of our internal split, where we take the beautiful and whole untapped potential of ourselves and divide it into parts to please others. We bring the parts of us people value closer to the surface and bury the parts that make us feel like a burden.

Instead of learning to feel safe to be who we are, we learn only it's safe to be who others need us to be. It's through returning to our essence and nurturing our "acorns," that we begin to see the depth of who we truly are; and to do this we need to unlearn some of the conditions we've been taught.

UNLEARNING AND HAPPINESS

A significant part of our journey in healing our past is unlearning that our worthiness of love and belonging is not conditional. Our worth is not dependent on our grades, measured by our successes, or quantified by how amenable we are. We do not have to be "more" or "less" of anything to be worthy, we exist and that's enough. We are worthy of love and belonging just as we are. When we return to our essence, we become whole and experience the freedom to allow ourselves to be deeply seen for who we are.

This journey of self-worth brings with it the realization that we're not lost, or broken, nor do we need to "find ourselves," as if our true selves were hiding behind a bush in a bizarre game of hide and seek. The treasure we've been searching for all along is there, it's just buried. It's resting beneath the limiting beliefs that we're not good enough, it's under the social conditioning of fear and people-pleasing. As we begin to remove the conditioning put there by others, we return to the essence of our presence that rests patiently at our core. We come home to who we are, keep our fingers close to our souls, evolving into who we were meant to be, and deepening the meaning in our lives.

This departure from our past involves a process that psychologists refer to as reparenting. Reparenting is where we learn to become the mother of all our parts, giving ourselves what we needed but didn't receive as

We do not have to be "more" or "less" of anything to be worthy, we exist and that's enough.

children. It's through reparenting that we create a safe space so that we as adults can teach ourselves how to hold our essence and live authentic, purposeful lives.

This process of unlearning and returning to who we truly are is part of the development of the evolving self. As psychologist Carl Jung writes, "Thoroughly unprepared, we take the step into the afternoon of life. Worse still, we take this step with the false presupposition that our truths and our ideals will serve us as hitherto. But we cannot live the afternoon of life according to the program of life's morning."[17] In my personal experience, the afternoon of life offers a magical new beginning that brings a wave of deep inner peace and paves the road for the life you feel called to live, rather than the one you were taught to reside in. The afternoon ushers in a new chapter of which you are the author, the guardian of your essence. It's inner happiness in its purest form.

EXERCISE

Self-reparenting

Self-reparenting involves becoming the mother of all your aspects, nurturing your inner child, and providing yourself with the words a younger version of yourself needed to hear. As you move through this process try to reduce any judgment or blame toward your parents or guardians. They often did the best with the skills they had.

AWARENESS: Bring awareness to the recurring patterns that are causing problems in your life. This can be lack of boundaries, conflict in relationships, not encouraging yourself to achieve what you are capable of, or any number of other issues.

UNRAVEL: Once you can observe your external behavior, follow the thread back to the internal belief you hold that is causing these patterns to manifest (e.g. people will leave me if I say no). You may find it helpful to examine how you learned this belief. Think back to what you were taught at school or how this belief appeared at home.

REPLACE: Now that you can see this belief was learned, it's time to reparent this aspect of yourself. Ask yourself what's more empowering to believe? How can you make it safe for that part of you to express how you really feel? What do you wish you would have been taught as a child that you can learn now?

REVEAL: Gradually put this new belief into practice (e.g. by saying no to others). Notice how whilst this initially feels uncomfortable, it's now more authentically aligned to who you are and how you feel.

OUT WITH THE OLD, IN WITH THE NEW

FIRING AND WIRING NEW BELIEFS

---

*"Our only limitations are
those we set up in our own minds."*

—Napoleon Hill

T he lack of belief in our potential can cause a flurry of negative feelings, including unhappiness, anxiety, and frustration. Whether we've grown to believe we can't speak in public, make new friends easily, be healthy, manage money, or find love, our beliefs can place unhelpful limits on our lives and happiness.

However, psychologists have found that it is possible to diminish our "can't do" attitude and choose more empowering beliefs that can positively influence our present and shape our future.

BELIEFS LINKING YOUR PAST, PRESENT, AND FUTURE

Psychologists have found we use past memories to formulate beliefs about our future performance. Research has found that even if we've never completed the task before, the level of confidence in our ability will be shaped by how well we perceived our performance in a similar situation.[18] While this can lead to growing levels of confidence in tasks we see ourselves to be good at, it can have a devastating impact on areas we perceive ourselves to be failing in.

This is because every time we perform the task we "can't do," we approach it with self-doubt, which strengthens our limiting thought pattern. In the long term, this may eventually lead to a self-fulfilling prophecy.

However, the good news is our beliefs are simply patterns of thinking that either serve or limit us in life, and we can change them. Indeed, changing belief systems by building new connections in our brains is now a widely accepted practice in interventions such as cognitive behavioral therapy and neuro-linguistic programming.

SCIENCE *of* BLISS

As Kathleen Taylor, a neuroscientist at Oxford University, explains, "Beliefs are mental objects in the sense that they are embedded in the brain. If you challenge them by contradiction, or just by cutting them off from the stimuli that make you think about them, then they are going to weaken slightly. If that is combined with a very strong reinforcement of new beliefs, then you're going to get a shift in emphasis from one to the other."[19]

Our limiting beliefs act like an invisible fence, separating the life we have from the life we desire. While these beliefs once protected us from harm, they can now have an adverse effect on our lives. We might feel stuck or frustrated, and may even alter our behavior to avoid certain situations.

While merely believing we can do something won't automatically make us better at it, it does enable us to act. In short, if we believe we are capable of change, then change can occur. But this requires more than motivational self-talk.

In order to really change our limiting beliefs, we need to challenge them, and that requires action. If you imagine moving towards something you "can't do," you'll notice a rise in discomfort and perhaps an increase in negative self-talk. That's where compassion comes in, to help give us the little push we need to overcome the hurdles of our limiting beliefs.

Dr. Kristin Neff, in an interview with the *New York Times*, explains: "Self-compassion is treating yourself with the same kindness, care, and concern you show a loved one."[20]

Accepting without judgment that we are flawed and imperfect humans builds our resilience and enables us to accept criticism. Both vital qualities to have when we step out of our comfort zone.

EXERCISE

Overcoming Limiting Beliefs

When we seek to overcome our limiting beliefs, cultivating the right level of challenge and compassion is key.

CHALLENGE: Challenging ourselves doesn't have to involve diving off the deep end. Indeed, psychologists use a technique called enactive self-mastery to improve the belief in our capabilities.

Enactive self-mastery is breaking a big task into smaller, more achievable parts. As you complete each task, you gradually build up the confidence that you "have what it takes."[21] For example, you might start with planning your presentation, then writing it, then practicing it alone in your room, and so on. Breaking tasks down helps relieve you if you feel overwhelmed as you gradually integrate your skills and build up self-belief in your capabilities.

COMPASSION: As you challenge yourself, things will go wrong. You'll make mistakes and grow from them. During these times, it's natural to be critical—it's a survival mechanism. Just be gentle and think about what words you would say to a loved one in the same scenario.

THE FREEDOM OF FORGIVENESS

"Not forgiving is like drinking rat poison
and then waiting for the rat to die."

—*Anne Lamott*

I f we want to release the hold the past has over our happiness, forgiveness will likely play a pivotal role in our journey. I know it has in mine. Forgiveness, for me, has been a process without a timeline. It's taken a series of small steps to gradually loosen my connection between what happened in the past and the negative emotions I've attached to it.

Furthermore, forgiveness facilitated my mental "should have," "would have," "could have," "why me?" and "if only" scenarios to slowly lose their grip. When we forgive, we no longer need to channel our energy into attempting to fix or undo the past. And as we set ourselves free from the pull of the past, we're able to enjoy the present and create our future with greater ease. But before we start our process of forgiveness, let's clarify what it means.

SCIENCE *of* BLISS

A study by Dr. William H. Frey found that tears might be the body's way of ridding itself of stress hormones. In the study, he found that people who cried emotionally-induced tears (e.g. by watching something sad) had a higher protein content than those who cried tears just from cutting an onion. He concluded that crying releases stress chemicals created in the body and that's why we feel better after having a cry.[22]

WHAT IS FORGIVENESS?

While it sounds straightforward, forgiveness can be a confusing concept riddled with misconceptions. It's common to mistake forgiveness as a seal of approval that it was OK for our offender to mistreat us.

But forgiveness is not excusing the behavior of the other person. Instead, forgiveness is accepting what *did* happen as opposed to accepting *what* happened. Equally, when we forgive, it does not always mean we allow that person back into our lives. On the contrary, forgiveness often means not only releasing our anger but also the individual who caused it.

When we choose to start the process of forgiveness, we signal to the world and ourselves that we are stopping the hurt from the past to cause us to suffer in the present and future moments. Far from being a sign of weakness, forgiveness is an act of self-love and strength. Indeed, psychologists have found that opting not to forgive and choosing to harbor feelings of resentment, revenge, and hurt can negatively impact your relationships as well as your physical and mental health.

In contrast, the act of forgiveness is associated with higher self-esteem, happier moods, and better relationships. And the good news is you don't need to wait for an apology or an act of atonement to begin the process.

FORGIVENESS AND HAPPINESS

As Oprah Winfrey so beautifully summarizes, "Forgiving is giving up the hope that the past could be any different. It's letting go so the past does not hold you prisoner." Forgiveness is a very personal journey, so when you decide you're ready to embark on it, be extra gentle and compassionate with yourself on the days when the emotion of the past feels raw.

Remember, forgiveness can take time. But when you finally reach the point of acceptance that the past has happened, you'll be able to let go of the pain and create a space for happiness.

Psychologists have shown that forgiveness protects our happiness over time. In the short-term, our capacity for happiness increases because we minimize the feelings of negative emotions. And in the long-term, research has found that we experience more personal growth as we think and feel about the experience with a more positive perspective.[23]

> "Even a happy life cannot be without a measure of darkness, and the word 'happy' would lose its meaning if it were not balanced by sadness."
>
> —*Carl Jung*

EXERCISE

Writing to Forgive

This exercise is designed to open you up and start the journey to forgive. It's ideal for those struggling to verbalize their pain.

STEP 1—ACKNOWLEDGE THE PAIN: When someone has hurt us, there may be words that we feel we can't say to them, particularly if they're our parents or loved ones. A useful way to acknowledge your pain is to write a letter to them that you'll never send and no one else will ever read. Writing a letter gives you space to be completely honest, and as you write without judgment, you'll bring recognition to the pain caused.

STEP 2—A DIFFERENT PERSPECTIVE: Next, write a second letter, this time responding as if you are the person that hurt you (it could be your mom, dad, a friend, a partner, or a relative). As you write the letter, imagine being them and writing a reply from their perspective about what happened. Writing from a different perspective is proven to help build empathy, an emotion shown to support the process of forgiveness.

STEP 3—CREATE A POSITIVE AFFIRMATION: Writing a positive affirmation helps signal a new beginning. It could be "I am worthy of releasing my past and feeling the peace of forgiveness," or "I am willing to forgive and let the past go." Write your affirmation down and put it up as a visual reminder that the past is behind you. This could be placing a post-it note on your mirror or creating a screensaver on your phone. As you affirm and practice your forgiveness through your thoughts, you'll gradually let go of past grudges and grievances.

5 ways
TO SOOTHE YOUR PAST

1. TURN ANGER INTO PASSION AND CREATE POSITIVE CHANGE

Anger can be a powerful catalyst for change when it's converted into a passion. With the right intentions, our outrage over past wrongs in the present can create a better future. Passion can fuel creativity, art, innovation, and even business ideas. Consider how your past could help others.

2. FORGIVE YOURSELF FOR PAST MISTAKES

We've all got closets full of regrets and mistakes, but it's never too late to forgive yourself. Everyone messes up in life, but it doesn't mean we have to continually punish ourselves for what happened. Don't lose faith in yourself. You can't change what has happened, but you can use it to change yourself.

3. REVISIT THE GOOD BITS OF YOUR PAST

We have a natural tendency to focus on what was wrong in the past. Take time to wander down memory lane, look through old photos, listen to old songs you love, and talk about happier memories with loved ones.

4. LEARN FROM THE PAST

The past can help provide lessons in the future. A few years ago, I started to keep a book with a list of "lessons from the past." I revisit this book frequently and it helps me avoid (as much as possible) learning the same mistakes over and over again. One lesson is, "Don't change your personality just to be liked. This will cause you to make unstable and unhealthy friendships that will end up causing you pain."

5. IT'S OK NOT TO BE OK

Some of our traumas are so great that using phrases like "let go of the past," "move on," or "get over it" only serve to add insult to injury. It's OK not to be completely OK with your past. Grief, sadness, and pain may never go away entirely, but this does not mean you are broken. You can find a way to live a happy life alongside these emotions.

believe

IN YOUR

future

"Life can only be understood backwards,
but it must be lived forwards."

—Søren Kierkegaard

THE FUTURE IS THE SPACE OF POSSIBILITY AND
disaster, where in our minds, anything can happen.
Befriending our ability to see the best and the worst
is perhaps our greatest superpower.

We shouldn't fear our worst-case scenario mind.
When it's kept in check, it can keep us safe. Nor
should we dampen our wildest dreams of what we
could be, since they can motivate and move us
forward. Instead, we can blend both capabilities
and utilize each for the purposes they were intended
and make well-informed, bold, and brave choices
in the future.

THE COMFORT
CONUNDRUM

"The more you practice tolerating discomfort,
the more comfort you'll gain in your ability
to accept new challenges."

—*Amy Morin*

I often wonder what our ancestors would think of our comfortable lives. We escape the chilly weather gliding from heated cars into heated offices, mobile phones eradicate the small discomfort of waiting for someone to arrive, and food is delivered to our door at the click of a button. Comfort sells, the easier and less painful the better. But there's a hidden price we're paying.

In terms of personal growth, comfort keeps us stuck. We bob up and down above the surface of our potential, it might feel like we're moving but we're not really going anywhere. We drift through life engaging in the same destructive behavioral loops, because to face change can bring discomfort. It's too awkward to say no, too daunting to follow our purpose, too hard to keep pursuing what matters most, too much effort to create new habits. Sure, we know we should do it, but it feels safer to snuggle into the safe illusion that we'll start tomorrow.

Comfort feels safe and when we aren't familiar with discomfort, we will find every loophole to avoid exposing ourselves to it and remain blissfully unaware that it comes at the price of our future potential. There's no right time to step into discomfort, sometimes we just have to get tired of hearing ourselves say "one day," hold our nose, and plunge into the abyss.

DISCOMFORT AND HAPPINESS

As we move into the future, the greatest ally we can make is getting comfortable with discomfort. Discomfort is not pain or suffering, it's the uncomfortable challenging moments that are bearable but unpleasant. Discomfort is the bridge between us and our unrealized potential that we all must walk across. It's that feeling of being on the edge of something great, the pull of hope that urges us to persevere. This is when humans are at their best, when we accomplish extraordinary things, and we feel alive.

Discomfort is a necessary passage through the unknown, where we have to navigate the space in between, where what we desire isn't fully realized yet but still in the works. The more we can hone our ability to be uncomfortable, the more we stretch into the depths of our potential and show ourselves that we're capable of more than we thought possible. Take a moment to consider and reflect on the accomplishments you found most rewarding. Do you notice the role discomfort played as part of the process?

SCIENCE *of* BLISS

Our capacity to walk over the bridge of discomfort helps us manage our anxiety about things that have not happened and maintain our commitment to our visions. Research tends to support these observations, with psychologist Maya Tamir, PhD, noting "Happiness is more than simply feeling pleasure and avoiding pain. Happiness is about having experiences that are meaningful and valuable... All emotions can be positive in some contexts and negative in others, regardless of whether they are pleasant or unpleasant."[24]

EXERCISE

The Discomfort Zone

The more we build our tolerance for discomfort, the easier it becomes to manage. Our levels of discomfort are specific to us, so this is about tuning in to what is tolerable for you and edging in and out of discomfort with small steps. Building up our ability to bear discomfort helps us cultivate the resilience to take bold, meaningful action.

- In this exercise think of something in your future you desire but that scares you, then follow these steps.

- Notice how you feel: Where in your body is the feeling? If the anxiety level is too high, how can you reduce it? What's the smallest step you can take?

- Close your eyes and imagine yourself taking this small step. What does that do for you? How does your life improve as a result? Does it bring you further away or closer to your goals?

- Keeping your eyes closed, imagine if you don't move forward. How does that change things? What direction does that move your life in?

- Write down a mantra that you can use each day to comfort your discomfort, something like "I am safe to explore my potential," or "I trust the timing of my life."

Our inner happiness is a lantern that rests within us. Sometimes it shines bright and other times it's a mere flicker, but it's always there to guide us through even the darkest of times. As we pay greater attention to our light, we begin to notice people, places, activities, and thought patterns that make us shine and those that dim us down. The more we're able to recognize our happiness, the more we can see its ability to guide us.

UNCERTAINTY'S
ILLUSION

"When you become comfortable with uncertainty,
infinite possibilities open up in your life."

—*Eckhart Tolle*

f the present moment had an archenemy, it would be uncertainty. When everything is going well, and life feels under control, uncertainty can swoop in like an evil villain and snatch our happiness as its hostage. And its superpower of creating fear-based illusions is impressive.

When uncertainty swoops in, nothing in our external world has changed. We're the same person at the same moment. It's the arrival of our inner fears over an uncertain future that changes the filter through which we see the world and alters our perception of reality.

Uncertainty uproots us from the present and thrusts our minds into various imaginary future worst-case scenarios, which, despite only being based on our overactive imagination, can feel very real. Like the flick of a switch, uncertainty can transform us from logical and calm into an anxious ball of worry that desperately craves guarantees over unpredictable future outcomes. When we're grappling with uncertainty, it can feel challenging to reconnect with the present moment and choose happiness.

ACTION AND ACCEPTANCE

When life is changing, we can swing between the extremes of either exerting excessive control or shrugging off our ability to take any action and allowing ourselves to free fall into the unknown. But the uncertainty sweet spot comes when action and acceptance merge in the present moment.

Let's say, for example, you're facing uncertainty over your job role as a result of an organizational restructuring. You've been in the position for a few years and financially you can't afford to lose your job.

In this scenario, the action you might take is to update your resume, contact recruitment agencies, refresh your interview skills, and fill out some job applications. Acceptance comes from merging the outcome of your actions. For instance, once you've completed the interview, you bring acceptance that it's over and the decision of the hiring manager is outside your control.

For me, I think the serenity prayer by American theologian Reinhold Niebuhr offers the most straightforward and wise words of advice in times of uncertainty. It encourages us to have the serenity to accept the thing we cannot change, the courage to change the things we can, and the wisdom to know the difference.

In times of uncertainty, the most helpful course of action is to trust the process and trust yourself in the process. If uncertainty is looming in your

happy
TIP

Handling uncertainty doesn't mean switching off our alarmist thinking entirely. On the contrary, living in delusion is just as dangerous as living in fear. It's useful to gather the facts, weigh our options, and keep our thoughts rational so we can make well-informed choices. Critical thinking can be an important tool in times of change and assist us in assessing multiple options.

life, try to find a moment of silence and ask yourself: "Where do I need to take action and where do I need to bring acceptance?"

UNCERTAINTY AND HAPPINESS

Our quest to transform the unknown into the known is a valuable human quality that has enabled us to thrive. We've used the power of uncertainty to drive technological innovations, pioneer medical breakthroughs, and discover new countries.

However, our fear of the unknown can reduce our level of everyday happiness and prevent us from taking action toward the future.

One surprisingly straightforward technique to help us outsmart uncertainty is writing. Psychologist James Pennebaker and his colleagues found through their research that individuals who write about traumatic events (typically for fifteen minutes over three consecutive days) can experience remarkable long-term benefits.[25] The researchers found that through writing, people were able to make sense of the unknown and take meaning from adverse events happening in their lives.

SCIENCE *of* BLISS

Research has shown that those with a low tolerance for uncertainty will experience more negative emotions such as anxiety and low mood, and feel less resilient.[26] Furthermore, psychologists have demonstrated that in times of uncertainty, our reactions are more intense, the low moods feel very low, and the highs feel very high.[27]

EXERCISE

Writing to Ease Uncertainty

Writing can help ease uncertainty. Take a pen and paper and write down your answers to these questions. Notice how you feel a greater sense of where you need to take action and where you need to practice acceptance.

During this exercise, let go of your emotions and just write without giving concern to spelling or grammar.

- What fear is driving your uncertainty?

- What action could you take to improve this situation?

- What areas are outside of your control? Where do you need to bring more acceptance?

- If a loved one was in this scenario, what advice would you offer them?

- What meaning can you take from this scenario?

- What lesson is this experience presenting that can help your inner growth?

BEFRIENDING FEAR

"May your choices reflect your hopes, not your fears."

—Nelson Mandela

We all have a collection of "one day I'd love to" stories in which we follow our dreams, have incredible experiences, and make an impact. In this wondrous "one day" world of possibility, we live life to its fullest potential. But leaving the comfort of this imaginary world and pulling your dreams into reality takes courage. As we transfer our aspirations from "one day" to "now," one of the biggest threats we'll face is our own fear.

Fear can be such a strong emotion that it can swallow up a hopeful thought before it has the opportunity to bloom into action. Faced with fear, many of us tuck our dreams safely in the comfort of our imagination, waiting for the "right time." As a result, fear keeps life small and safe and prevents us from ever really knowing the rich, textured, sublime adventure that awaits us on the other side of it.

WALKING WITH FEAR

If you decide to pursue a goal or a dream that's personally compelling to you, fear is going to be with you on the journey.

Take a moment to picture your fear as your over-cautious, over-protective, possibly has a job in health and safety friend. Let's call your fear Fred. Now, Fred's positive intention is to protect you from harm. And Fred believes that the best way to do that is to interrupt your thoughts and sleep to tell you your dreams are silly, that people will laugh at you, that you'll spectacularly fail, and nothing will go your way. Fred will do his best to convince you to never take action and, therefore, never come to harm.

However, if we are to choose to savor the joy, happiness, and divine possibilities that come from venturing toward what matters most to us, then we need to learn how to keep fear under control.

Contrary to popular belief, the most successful people don't avoid or suppress fear's presence, but learn to journey with it. In an interview, psychologist Stanley Rachman, a leading expert on fear from the University of British Columbia, contends that brave people are not numb to danger or discomfort; they feel and acknowledge fear, and refuse to allow it to dominate their behavior.[28]

If fear is coming on the journey regardless, then psychology research suggests that learning how to walk with it rather than run from it is critical to both our happiness and success.

FEAR AND HAPPINESS

Fear is natural. It unites us as human beings and, in theory, our fear should lend itself to happiness. After all, its primary function is to protect us against life-threatening events. So why does it interfere with our happiness and sound its alarm when we want to try a non-life-threatening task like perform a new activity, visit a new country, or make a career change?

Professor of psychology and neuroscience at Duke University, Ahmad Hariri, explains that our brains are equipped with a highly sensitive yet primitive threat detector. Speaking in an interview with the *New York Times*, he observes this can cause us to "drive ourselves nuts worrying about things because we have too much time and don't have many real threats on our survival, so fear gets expressed in these really strange, maladaptive ways."[29] If we want to minimize fear and boost our happiness, the research suggests we must acknowledge and accept our fear as opposed to avoiding it.

EXERCISE

Walking with Fear

Learning how to walk with our fear means we need to learn how to listen to it (sometimes it has valid points) and reassure it. When we learn to walk with our fear, we accept its presence but not its control.

SAY HELLO: When fear shows up, avoid pushing it down by accepting its presence. Simply saying, "Hi fear," enables us to label the feeling as a word. There is a growing body of research that shows this simple act can decrease the impact the emotion has on us.[30]

LISTEN: Objectively listen to what fear has to tell you as if you were hearing the concerns of a friend. This cognitive distance enables us to remove ourselves from fear's dialogue and objectively decide how to move forward (e.g., are we taking on too much of a challenge that we don't yet have the skills for?).

REASSURE: Take time to speak kindly to your fear, reassure it that you are in control and have all the resources you need to move forward. Reassurance will help take you out of any fight-or-flight response, leaving you feeling more calm and able to make better choices.

STEP INTO YOUR FUTURE WITH AWE

"The world is full of magic things,
patiently waiting for our senses to grow sharper."

—William Butler Yeats

We face the future united in our uncertainty, and it can be daunting. But in the words of Joseph Campbell, "Awe is what enables us to move forward." Awe is the positive goosebump feeling we experience when we sense we are part of something greater than ourselves.

Perhaps you've felt awe watching a beautiful sunset, seeing a moving performance, marveling at a nature documentary, or staring up at the stars. Awe is an essential collective emotion that plays a pivotal role in our shared future happiness.

WE ARE ALREADY AMIDST AWE

If you currently have dirty dishes piled up, a massive to-do list, and an anxiety-fueled mind that's racing a million miles per hour with real and imaginary problems, it can be hard to feel you are amidst awe (or anywhere near it for that matter). While children experience awe with ease as they marvel at the world, as busy adults who can find it hard to peer up from our devices, life has become awe-deprived.

But awe is all around us. Consider the sheer notion that we have a one in four hundred trillion chance of being born. Or that we're currently being weighed down by an invisible force called gravity on a planet that is spinning at roughly one thousand miles per hour, yet we can't feel it. That's enough to give me goosebumps. As the author of *The Body*, Bill Bryson, writes, "Think of it: there is enough of you to leave the solar system...You are in the most literal sense cosmic."[31] Returning to awe can bring a return to happiness and ease our future fears.

AWE AND HAPPINESS

Research has shown that when we experience awe it can boost our mood, well-being, and life satisfaction.[32] It can even expand our sense of time, with one study finding that people who felt awe were less impatient. Researchers wrote that "awe-eliciting experiences might offer one effective way of alleviating the feeling of time starvation that plagues so many people in modern life."[33] And the benefits don't stop there.

In a fascinating research study, Michiel van Elk and his colleagues at the University of Amsterdam examined how our brain changes when we experience awe. Their results suggested that awe might help pull us out of worry and rumination by connecting us to the larger world.[34] All of these benefits mean we can approach the future being happier, more satisfied, less worried, and more patient.

But the benefits of experiencing awe aren't just restricted to us. Psychologists have shown that when we feel a sense of awe, we are also more generous and connected.[35]

happy TIP

If you struggle to access activities such as nature appreciation, music, or art, the good news is research indicates that watching a nature video or listening to music at home, will elicit awe.[36]

EXERCISE

Creating an Awe-some Future

As you move into the future, integrating time for awe can promote your happiness and well-being. Here are two areas where people experience awe and suggestions on how to integrate it.

NATURE, MUSIC, AND ART: Awe is most commonly felt when we experience nature, music, or art. Think about how you can create more time to integrate these activities. It can be as simple as a walk in nature at lunch or checking out the local music and art scene.

FINDING AWE IN OTHER PEOPLE: We can feel in awe of other people and their contribution to the world. These stories can be an incredible reminder of what humans can achieve. Consider how you could connect with or listen to inspirational people. Perhaps it's through local meetups, listening to podcasts, or reading autobiographies. Where can you find a sense of awe about what humans have the potential to achieve?

TAKING MICRO-STEPS TOWARD MEANING

> "If you don't go after what you want, you'll never have it. If you don't ask, the answer is always no. If you don't step forward, you're always in the same place."
>
> —*Nora Roberts*

Purpose comes in many different forms, we can have more than one, and it can change over time. Purpose can be anything from making people happy with your cakes, writing, raising a family, or setting up a business.

Our purpose may be highly individual, but one consistent characteristic it holds is that it's a feeling. It's an indescribable feeling knowing that you are meant to do that thing. Purpose is the why that pulls us forward into the future even though we know the journey might not always be easy. But if you don't know your purpose, where do you even begin?

It's understandable that when we feel a bit low or lost, adding "find my purpose" to the list of things we can compulsively worry about can make us hide under our bed covers. For many of us, finding our purpose can feel like the enormous elephant in life we'd all rather ignore until later.

However, by rethinking what's meant by finding our purpose, we can shrink its enormity and still ensure that we reap the tremendous happiness benefits it can bring. If you feel overwhelmed by finding your purpose, it can be helpful to think of it like going on a treasure hunt.

RETHINKING PURPOSE

On a treasure hunt, our overall goal is to find the hidden treasure, and it would be boring if the hunt consisted of just one clue that brought us to the end. After all, the joy of a treasure hunt is in the process. The story we tell about solving a treasure hunt mainly comprises of the fun and frustration of figuring out each clue to the elation of suddenly knowing as you race to the end. If you listen to anyone describe the story of their purpose, you are likely to notice a similar pattern. Their story might end on a big "Aha!" But it's predominantly a series of small ohs as they followed clues that eventually lead toward their purpose. And the clues are already in front of you.

When it comes to finding our purpose, the journey starts when we're ready to begin. And we don't have to wait until life is great or we have everything figured out. Many of the most significant turning points that led toward purpose were born out of uncertainty, pain, and feeling lost.

As author Elizabeth Gilbert so eloquently summarizes, "The most interesting moment of a person's life is what happens to them when all their certainties go away. Then who do you become? And then what do you look for? That's the moment when the universe is offering up an invitation, saying, 'Come and find me.'"

Perhaps the resistance you feel in your life may turn out to be your greatest teacher. Maybe you'll use what you learned to inspire others, create a new product, or pursue a different career. We are the meaning makers of our own life.

Wherever we are in life, our purpose is to be fully present with that moment, aligning our actions with our intention of what we desire in the future. Our purpose (or purposes) is ready to start revealing itself when we are willing to accept the invitation to find it.

> *... the joy of a treasure hunt is in the process.*

Purpose gives us a sense of meaning, which has been linked to greater work enjoyment, life satisfaction, and happiness.[37] And purpose does more than impact our mental health. One recent study revealed that people with a strong life purpose live longer.[38]

But don't be blinded by the bright lights of purpose. A common misconception is that having a purpose means we all have to do something big in the world, like solving climate change or winning an Oscar. A recent study into the purpose of life by psychologists Matthew Scott and Adam Cohen found that we can find purpose in fulfilling some of our small basic needs, like caring for our family or finding a romantic partner.

SCIENCE *of* BLISS

Purpose comes in many forms and as one of the authors, Matthew Scott, notes, the benefits to purpose are felt in the journey. He says in an interview, "Previous research shows that goal pursuit, not contemplation, predicts purpose in life. If life is feeling purposeless, putting one foot in front of the other toward the pursuit of hardwired social needs might restore purpose."[39]

FINDING YOUR PURPOSE

Like every treasure hunt, you begin where you are and move forward from there. Finding our purpose involves taking small micro-steps and reconnecting with our passions. To kickstart the process, use these journal prompts to help you reconnect with your joy and find clues to your purpose.

- What gives you joy?

- What did you enjoy doing as a kid?

- What experiences would you like to have in life?

- How could you use your skills, passion, or knowledge to help others?

- What interests you?

Daily Delights

What is purpose? Purpose is the passionate sense that our potential can be used for the benefit of something greater than ourselves. Purpose gives meaning to life's swirling chaos, offering an almost cosmic clarity that we're meant to be here.

Purpose and the possibility of finding it are what make life interesting. And we must keep walking toward it. If we stop for too long, we risk being frozen by indecision at the endless directions branching out in front of us. If purpose is calling you to just put one step in front of the other and try your best to manage. Its enemy is self-doubt.

HAVE A LITTLE PATIENCE

"Patience is not the ability to wait,
but the ability to keep a good attitude while waiting."

—*Joyce Meyer*

In our quick-fix culture, patience can run low when it comes to cultivating happiness. Add in a fiercely optimistic self-help industry promising untold happiness at the flick of a switch, and it's unsurprising that so many of us prematurely ditch our gratitude journaling or meditation apps.

It may not be the message that sells, but genuine change isn't an overnight process. I feel that making some simple, subtle changes to the structure of everyday life can over time, lead to significant change. But the real challenge lies in the dedication and patience to make that steady transformation.

Happiness has become a status symbol, and as a result, the visibility of our human struggle has become less and less. Social media feeds are flooded with everyone living their best life, as we spend more time getting the perfect picture than enjoying the moment. But our cultural obsession with being seen to be happy might be what's making us unhappy.

Accepting that life will sometimes be tough can unite and help us be more patient with our own happiness. There is power in walking into your future, knowing bad days will come and that they will pass. It helps us weather life's storms to know that tomorrow is another day, that you're not a failure, and you haven't got it all wrong. You're just a human being trying to make the best out of life.

In these moments, be patient with yourself and know there are so many good times and happy memories waiting for you on the other side. When we choose to be happy, we're making a decision to accept that life will be problematic but that we'll always have the ability to shift our perspective to ease its impact.

SCIENCE *of* BLISS

Perceiving the rest of the world appear to be happy when we feel low can be an isolating experience. It's easy to feel singled out by the universe and wonder what we have done to deserve to feel this way. However, despite what social media might portray, the statistics show that anxiety and depression are on the rise, with forty million adults in America suffering from an anxiety disorder (that's 18.1% percent of the population).[40]

Patience is defined by psychologists as the "propensity to wait calmly in the face of frustration or adversity."[42] It's a unique blend of acceptance and hope that enables us to move forward.

But there is no such thing as a patient person. Research shows patience is a trait we can develop and that can act as a buffer against negative emotions.[43] Perhaps one of the oldest and strongest traditions of instilling this sense of patience to weather life's difficult journey is Buddhism.

In Buddhism, practicing patience not only means the acceptance of negative emotions but also optimistically re-evaluating the challenging times that cause us suffering. While this area needs more research, a recent study concluded that the Buddhist approach to patience was a positive psychological characteristic related to authentic, durable happiness. This type of patience can keep us centered and focused in challenging times (because we anticipated it) and happier (because we are less disappointed or discouraged).

happy TIP

Some psychologists have suggested that having a patient acceptance of life's frustrations can make us less likely to give up our goals or act at the wrong time.[41]

EXERCISE

Practicing Patience

Patience is a trait we can learn and develop. Here are three tips to help you cultivate patience and accept that life will be frustrating while remaining hopeful of the future.

MANAGE YOUR EXPECTATIONS: Most of us would agree that it's an unrealistic expectation for a novice runner to wake up and decide to run a marathon next week. Yet we continually impose high expectations on how much we and others should be able to achieve in short time frames. High expectations can lead to overscheduling, burnout, and stress.

It can be helpful to take a step back and reflect on whether your expectations are overly ambitious. Are you too hard on yourself? Would it be more useful to rest and recharge than to push forward?

ZOOM OUT: When setbacks pull you off course, it can be easy to lose patience and tell ourselves it's not worth it. If your patience is running low, pause and zoom out. Try viewing the setback in the bigger picture to gain perspective.

ASK FOR HELP: When we are facing a challenging time, we also need people to be a little more patient with us. It can be helpful to reach out to those you trust and explain how you feel. This way, if you are distant or frustrated, you've given them opportunity to show a bit more patience toward you.

YOU ARE ENOUGH

"If you need everyone else to approve of you before you approve of yourself you will be waiting forever."

—Matt Haig

We all have a need to be seen, heard, and to feel worthy in the world. And as we forge our path through life, many of us learn to temporarily satisfy this need by pleasing, perfecting, and performing.

Over time, we perceive happiness and self-worth to exist outside of us as things that have to be earned. Yet no matter what we do, no amount of recognition ever feels good enough for long enough. A sense of unworthiness can hold us back from pursuing our future, as we take up residence in life's waiting room.

We put life on hold, waiting until we drop ten pounds, meet our partner, or get a great job, telling ourselves that once we achieve that standard, then we will be worthy of living fully. If we could all work on just one thing that would move us forward the most in life, it would be self-worth.

THE TROUBLE WITH NOT FEELING ENOUGH

Not understanding how to give self-worth to ourselves can become an addiction. Our minds become a painful, dizzying mix of thoughts about whether we're good enough, doing enough, and achieving enough.

To soothe our pain, we seek out validation, praise, and status, or distract ourselves by being too busy to give ourselves that sense of being important. All of which temporarily numbs the pain, but it doesn't take long before the effects wear off and we start the cycle all over again.

Like any addiction, this behavior has its consequences. Eventually, the physical and mental impact catches up with us, manifesting in anxiety, burnout, perfectionism, envy, and insecurity. But there are ways to stop tormenting ourselves and halt the cycle.

When we show compassion and kindness toward ourselves by telling ourselves "I am loved. I am worthy. I can do this. I am enough," the addiction's hypnotic hold starts to lose its control over us. It's in this sacred space of worthiness that we have the freedom to choose whether we listen to the narrative of "I am not enough" or choose a different one. I believe we should all start our journey into the future with the belief that we are enough.

If you have ambitions and dreams, you should reach for those shiny gold stars of achievement. But reach for them for the memories, experiences, and learning they provide and not as a means to prove yourself worthy to be in the world.

You do not lack anything. You do not need to be perfect to be worthy of love, and you don't need to earn your place in the world. You, just as you are now at this moment and in the next, are already enough. Engage with the world from this place of worth and notice how it changes.

> *You do not lack anything. You do not need to be perfect to be worthy of love, and you don't need to earn your place in the world.*

It's tempting and often easier to chase worthiness rather than learn how to cultivate it for ourselves. After all, it feels good when we are praised, and indeed, research shows that when we achieve external goals that increase our self-esteem, we gain the short-term benefits of increased happiness and decreased anxiety. So, what's the harm?

Well, psychologists Jennifer Crocker and Katherine McKnight from the University of Michigan liken the temporary happiness high we experience from external validation to that of the feel-good rush we get from sugar, saying it's "tasty but not nutritious." In their research, Crocker and McKnight warn that seeking our self-worth from others or achievements in the long-term can result in stress, anxiety, and depression, as well as negatively impact our physical health.[44]

If we genuinely want to be happy in the long run, then the ability to cultivate our own sense of feeling enough is a vital part of the happiness puzzle.

Daily Delights

Ask yourself how unworthiness shows up in your life by using the following journal prompts:

- What do you tell yourself about your self-worth?
- How do you prove your worth to others?
- Are these thoughts and behaviors serving you?
- Is this pattern of behavior making you happy?

E X E R C I S E

The Art of Self-Compassion

Our ability to feel enough is a precious psychological resource that we must continually nurture throughout our lives, and research suggests one of the most effective ways to do this is by learning the art of self-compassion.[45] Here are three suggestions to help kickstart your journey.

ACCEPTING IMPERFECTION: When we accept that we and life are imperfect, we can treat ourselves with greater self-kindness and reduce the need for constant positive evaluations from others. The simple reminder and acceptance that mistakes, setbacks, and hardships are things that connect, rather than isolate us from the rest of humanity, can help cultivate a more compassionate approach toward ourselves.

SPEAK WITH COMPASSION: We are often our own worst critic, and the voice inside our head can berate us for even the smallest of mistakes. When we face hardships or feel inadequate, learning to soothe ourselves like we would a best friend is a critical skill.

SELF-VALIDATE: Begin to find ways to validate yourself by exploring how you can celebrate your own successes. Take a moment to reflect on the following questions: How can I give myself the praise that I need? How can I begin to show myself it's safe to prioritize my needs? How could I celebrate my small successes each day?

ASK YOURSELF: How can I give myself the praise that I need? What ways can I show myself that I am worthy?

5 *ways*
TO MOVE FORWARD
INTO THE FUTURE

1. CREATE A VISION BOARD

Creating a vision board can be a powerful visual motivator to move us toward our goals. A vision board is a collection of images and quotes that inspire you to achieve your goals. How you choose to create your vision board—digitally or on paper—is entirely up to you. Just make sure it's somewhere visible.

2. DON'T BE AFRAID
TO PAUSE AND THINK

If you aren't sure what you want in the future or can't decide if you are moving forward in the right direction, don't be afraid to take time out. Stopping to pause and think critically can be beneficial. Give yourself permission to be OK with not knowing what comes next and work from there.

3. THINK FLEXIBLY

It's great to have specific plans and targets, but because life can change quickly, we need our thinking to be flexible. When circumstances change, thinking in imaginative, non-logical ways can help us imagine creative solutions.

4. HAVE RATIONAL HOPE

Glimmers of hope in the future in dispiriting times can light the way forward. As humans, we can always have hope. Not the excessive hope that tells us there isn't a problem, but a rational hope that accepts things are bad while looking for possibilities and guidance to find a way out of troubled times. This type of hope can help us stay grounded and grow at the same time.

5. GO AT YOUR OWN PACE AND FOLLOW YOUR OWN PLAN

We are each unique and it's important that we move into the future at our own pace, following our own plan. Don't be hurried along or dragged back by those around you. Find what works for you and trust your ability to navigate life.

enjoy

YOUR

present

"Learning to live in the present
moment is part of the path to joy."

—*Sarah Ban Breathnach*

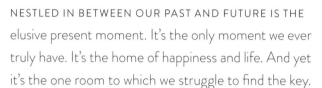

NESTLED IN BETWEEN OUR PAST AND FUTURE IS THE elusive present moment. It's the only moment we ever truly have. It's the home of happiness and life. And yet it's the one room to which we struggle to find the key.

While the door to our past swings open with a gentle nudge and our future fears are so eager to invite us in, the present moment and the sublime happiness it offers takes effort, awareness, and discipline to unlock.

One large-scale study found that people spend forty-seven percent of their time thinking about other things as opposed to being fully present in what they're doing.[46] It's fair to say the majority of us could use a helping hand to understand how to be more fully present.

THIS IS YOUR LIFE
REGAINING CONTROL
OF YOUR INNER NARRATIVE

"There are times in our lives when we have to realize our
past is precisely what it is, and we cannot change it.
But we can change the story we tell ourselves about it,
and by doing that, we can change the future."

—Eleanor Brown

We make sense of our lives through the stories we tell about them. The story of your life, much like any fictional story, is likely to have villains, plot twists, tragedies, and triumphs. It's through stories that we're able to create a sense of meaning from life. Our ability to construct an inner narrative that connects our past, future, and present is a universal human quality.

Psychologists refer to our natural ability to tell stories as our narrative identity and define it as "a selective and subjective account of how one came to be the person one currently is."[47] Most importantly, psychologists stress that how we construct our story plays an essential part in determining our level of happiness.

TUNING INTO YOUR STORY

It's often easier to observe other people's narratives of the past than to see our own. It's easy to spot our friend with the victim narrative who repeatedly tells the story of how "it always seems to happen to her" as she jumps from one chapter of drama to the next. And to recognize our "everything happens for a reason" friend, who takes life's downturns and transforms them into opportunities, finding glimmers of hope even in their darkest times.

As an observer, we can see how a simple shift in perspective changes the experience of each of our friends. However, our over-involvement in our own story can make it hard to tune into the narrative that's running in our head.

As you tune into your story, notice your perspective widen, enabling you to step outside of the role of character and firmly place yourself as the author of your narrative. Assuming the role of an author can help us regain control of our personal story, and we can come to experience our constant ability to edit, refine, and turn the page to start a new chapter.

Daily Delights

Whether you feel negative emotions about the recent or distant past, take a journal or paper and write your answers to these prompts, noticing how they help you tune into and observe the story of the past you are creating.

* What am I telling myself about this situation?

* When I tell this story, how does it make me feel?

* How is this story serving me?

EXERCISE

Inner Narrative and Happiness

Our internal narrative is inexplicably linked to happiness, and thanks to research by psychologists, we now have a greater understanding behind the science of structuring our story for happiness.[48]

This is not about self-delusion, in-depth analysis of linguistic patterns from people who've experienced trauma and gone on to create meaningful and happy lives shows us how we can do the same. We may not have had control over the external events that happened to us, but we do have the internal control to shape the story we allow it to tell.

FIND THE MEANING: Research has shown that people who found meaning or gained an increased understanding about themselves from a particular turning point in their lives demonstrated higher levels of optimism.[49] How can I help others learn from the experience I've had? How could this empower me to create change in the future? What good can I allow to come from this?

As you reflect on a negative story of the past, it can be helpful to find some meaning. Ask yourself: What lessons could I learn from this situation? What insights are there to be had? What did it teach me?

ADD SOME REDEMPTION: Stories of redemption begin with the bad and end with the good. If you've had a bad experience, try to reflect on the good that it brought to your life, however small. It could be the strength it gave you, or how it shaped the person you are or are becoming for the better.

Stories that have redemption in them can have a powerful effect. For example, one study found that adults in Alcoholics Anonymous who told a redemptive story about their last drink were more likely to report staying sober for four months compared to participants whose narrative did not contain the feature of redemption.[50]

I have incorporated redemption into stories in my own life, particularly around ending unhealthy friendships. It's still painful to recall the memories of how I was treated, and those relationships gnawed at my already low self-worth. But whenever I reflect on the push it gave me to find my own voice and to set firm boundaries, I am reminded of how valuable this experience was. Now, I'm strangely both hurt and grateful for those experiences. It helped me to evolve from a people pleaser to someone who strongly values their own worth.

TELL A GROWTH STORY: Stories of how we have positively grown from our experiences are linked with higher levels of well-being and happiness. As you reflect on your past, think about how you have developed. How did the experience help you grow as a person? How has the past helped you make better decisions about the future?

I have seen this technique powerfully impact the lives of people I've worked with. These people have turned burnout from work, social anxiety, addiction, and failed marriages into growth stories. It can be so empowering when we decide for ourselves, "This isn't how it ends. This is actually where my story really begins."

JUST FOR FUN

"We don't stop playing because we grow old;
we grow old because we stop playing."

—*George Bernard Shaw*

'm not really sure at what point we come out of the cocoon of play and emerge as serious adults with long to-do lists. When we're younger, adulthood is often revered as the point when we'll finally get to do whatever we want.

As a child, I used to imagine that my adult life would be a bit like that of the character Josh in the classic movie *Big*. (If you haven't seen *Big*, twelve-year-old Josh makes a wish on the Zoltar fortune-telling machine at a fairground to become a grown-up and it comes true). Like Josh, I'd imagined that grown-up Sarah would stay up late and have a trampoline in the living room and an abundance of cool toys.

In reality, life as a grown-up means I struggle to make time for play. The practical jobs, responsibilities, and obligations of life can overcrowd my diary and my mind, slowly edging happiness out of the present. But when life feels overwhelming and the present moment feels hard to access, play offers us sanctuary and the release that we so desperately need.

PLAYTIME

Play is when we engage in activity for the purpose of joy with little concern over the outcome. And what creates that feeling of play will be unique to each of us. It might be hosting a game night, playing football, taking part in a murder mystery evening, skateboarding, surfing, dancing, acting, or cooking.

But when we feel low or just a bit off, the extra effort required to create room for play can feel like a stretch too far.

After all, it's a much easier choice to numb our negative emotions with our televisions or phones than to get creative about where we can find play. Nonetheless, various pieces of research indicate that summoning that extra energy to invest in play can pay off, reaping immediate and long-term benefits.

PLAY AND HAPPINESS

Play is an integral part of the happiness equation. It's proven to reduce stress and is associated with higher levels of life satisfaction.[51] What's more, the benefits of play are almost immediate, given that we're more likely to access the psychological state of flow.

Flow is when our action and awareness merge, totally engaging us in the present moment. It's in the state of flow that people report "being in the zone." It's where our sense of time is distorted—it speeds up or slows down—and our sense of self, worries, and inner critic dissolve. Flow hits our inner voice's mute button by heavily investing our attention in the present.

Perhaps this escape from our overactive minds is one of the reasons why psychologists hail flow as the secret to happiness. Play can remind us, even if it's just for a few moments, that life can be light and enjoyable. It's a great choice to engage in the present moment and get out of our heads and into our lives.

E X E R C I S E

Establishing and Expanding Your Level of Play

This three-step process is a valuable starting point for establishing and expanding your current level of play.

Establishing and expanding our levels of play can feel awkward or even silly. I remember the resistance I felt at a seminar when the speaker suggested that we make more time for play. I recall rolling my eyes and whispering to a colleague beside me, "Sure thing, let's just get all our clients bouncing around on bouncy castles and all their worries will just fly away."

My resistance was triggered because the speaker had hit a nerve at the lack of play in my own life. I spent too much time in my head thinking serious adult thoughts and not enough time having fun and laughing. If you feel a similar resistance, that's OK. Play won't solve all your grown-up problems, but it will offer a brief, important opportunity to escape them for short time.

STEP 1: Rate the level of play in your life from one to ten (with one being "no play" and ten being "my life is full of play").

STEP 2: If you feel your play score could be higher, make a list of ten play activities. It's useful to think about activities where you find joy, feel "in the zone," lose track of time, or once enjoyed as a child. If you find it difficult to write ten, here are some suggestions that might help spark a few ideas:

- Host a game night
- Download interactive apps to play with others
- Make a visit to a board game café
- Dance, whether it's in a dance class or you are just dancing in the living room to some of your favorite songs
- Use websites like Meetup.com or Facebook to find events happening in your area
- Play sports like football, basketball, or tennis
- Get crafty with painting, knitting, drawing, or even an adult coloring book
- Try new gym classes
- Take an improv class or acting class
- Think about and revisit old childhood games you used to love to play like hide and seek or I-spy

STEP 3: Write down when and where next week you will create room for play. It can be as small as making five minutes a day to dance like no one's watching, or as big as pushing yourself out of your comfort zone with an improv class.

RELEASE YOUR JUDGEMENT

"Everyone seems to have a clear idea
of how other people should lead their lives,
but none about his or her own."

—*Paulo Coelho*

W e share the present moment with other people, and when they don't act in accordance with our expectations, it can disrupt our thoughts and dominate our conversations. A throwaway comment or a sour-toned email from a colleague is sometimes all it takes for us to pick up our judgment hammer and put other people's behavior on trial.

But we do this often at the expense of our own time and happiness by tormenting ourselves with a cascade of why questions. Why did they say that? Why did they do that? Why are they treating me like this? In the absence of the other person's defense, our brains construct elaborate subjective stories. Judging others consumes our thoughts and focus, and unnecessarily wastes energy. Like a happiness sponge, judgment can soak up not only our own happiness but the happiness of those around us. So understanding when it's best to drop the judgment hammer and let it go can help us create space for happiness in the present.

IS IT TRUE?

We like the world to make sense and for people to act in accordance with our norms and values. When people deviate from our invisible rules, it can feel difficult to get past. We find ourselves talking excessively to almost anyone, typically apart from the person involved, about what happened, seeking reasons and validation of our own values.

But in the process of telling our side of the story, we can distort the truth, mistakenly using a small part of the person's behavior to construct an entire picture of who they are. The surge of moral superiority that accompanies it can feel good.

In the past, I've slammed the hammer of judgment on people and found them guilty of being insensitive and selfish, only to later uncover deeper reasons for their behavior that came from a place of stress, hurt, and anxiety. It's in moments like these I wish I'd stepped outside my individualistic world, tried to understand the person's motivation, and seen the bigger picture. Taking this approach would have improved my happiness and afforded me the opportunity to improve theirs too.

Like a happiness sponge, judgment can soak up not only our own happiness but the happiness of those around us.

JUDGING OTHERS AND HAPPINESS

Human beings are hard-wired for connection and relationships are vital for everyone's well-being. However, inevitably in relationships, wires get crossed and conflict can occur. But it is possible to iron out our differences, and research indicates that empathy can help.[52]

Empathy helps us step off our moral soapbox and close the gap between our assumptions and reality. Even though it feels quicker and easier to judge, taking time to think about the other person's point of view can be extremely beneficial.

One way to cultivate empathy is to step into the other person's shoes, consider their point of view, and get a sense of their situation and what they might be thinking or feeling. Ask yourself: What assumptions have you made about this situation? What values and beliefs has the person challenged?

Know that enshrining someone in empathy doesn't mean we have to excuse the other person's behavior. If you feel someone did hurt your feelings or acted without care, then be assertive and take action where possible, setting clear boundaries for yourself.

happy TIP | Relationships play a huge role in our level of happiness. Knowing someone who makes you happy makes you 15.3 percent more likely to be happy. What's more, a happy friend of a friend will increase your happiness by 9.8 percent.[53]

EXERCISE

Rising Above Judgment

Our judgment of others was once a useful survival mechanism that would alert us to people who might harm us. But now our judgment can get in the way, negatively impacting the other person and affecting our own lives and happiness. If someone at work has stolen your ideas, your friend has been continually putting you down, or a loved one has been showing you a lack of respect, here are some tips to help you resolve it.

DIRECT COMMUNICATION: If we seek to understand someone else's behavior, it's logical that we go directly to them. However, for some, this can be easier said than done.

If you feel able to approach the person directly, remain calm and objective by using phrases like "I find this a tough conversation to have. But could you help me understand why...?" or "I'd like to understand more about (insert what happened). I don't know if you realized, but it caused me to feel (insert your feeling)."

Direct communication, however uncomfortable, allows the other person to share their story. You might find you're pleasantly surprised with how grateful the person is to share their version of events.

LET IT GO OR LET THEM GO: If you don't feel the explanation is enough and conflicts still arise, then you may feel it necessary to reflect on whether the relationship is one you need to end. Ending relationships can feel very difficult, especially if it's a close friend, partner, or family member. Each case is individual, but when it comes to toxic relationships, trust your gut and value your worth.

THE COMPARISON CATAPULT

"Comparison is the thief of joy."

—*Theodore Roosevelt*

---

omparison fuels feelings of unworthiness, unfairness, envy, and jealousy that catapult us out of the present moment and into the desert of inadequacy. Comparison can have the power to make our hearts sink and our minds wander in an instant. It leads us to question if we're doing enough or if we're good enough, and to ponder the perceived unfairness of why them and not us. When we're snared in the comparison trap, it's tempting to dish out criticism or silently wish for others to fail in an attempt to make us feel better.

Comparison is a complex emotion, and the opportunities to step into its catapult seem endless in our hyper-filtered, hyper-connected world. But taking the time to look at the cause of our comparison feelings can be very revealing.

YOU ARE ENOUGH

The evaluations of our lives against others' is often driven by the underlying fear that we are not enough. We convince ourselves that if we had what they have, then we would feel loved, validated, and accepted, and life would be complete.

The rise of the influencer has tapped into these fears and opened up a new marketing stream for watch brands, clothing ranges, and the diet industry to offer solutions to fill the void we feel. Comparison can gnaw at our self-esteem and make us hypercritical of ourselves and others. In these times, self-love and positive self-talk are crucial anecdotes as we gently remind ourselves that we are on our own unique journey. More than ever, we should remember the highlight reel of people's lives we see isn't the whole picture, but an unsustainable mirage of their best bits. We'll never really know the journey that person went on to get there, the struggles, hard work, self-doubt, and the feelings of inadequacy they faced along the way.

As you feel comparison take over your world and snatch your happiness, remember that you are enough; we all are. Another person's success doesn't devalue or take away anything from you, your life, and your journey.

COMPARISON AND HAPPINESS

Social comparison is a normal part of human behavior that's easy to fall into, but it takes effort to pull ourselves out from that bad habit. Interestingly, one of the main reasons why we compare ourselves with others is when we don't have objective clarity over our own goals. Studies have revealed that when we are clear on our own internal standards, we pay less attention to the performance of others and feel happier ourselves.

Contrastingly, when we're uncertain about our level of self-worth and abilities, we make more frequent social comparisons to gauge our performance.[54] Yet that's about as useful as trying to work out if you're taller than someone when you don't know your own height. Being in tune with our own internal barometer of success means understanding the answer to the question, "is this enough for me?"

EXERCISE

Managing Social Comparison

Social comparison is natural, but when it catapults you out of the present moment, here are some practical steps you can take to manage its impact.

STRANGERS AND SOCIAL MEDIA: A study found that people who follow fewer strangers on Instagram were associated with decreased depressive symptoms.[55]

If you wouldn't invite a stranger into your home who made you feel bad about your life, why let them into your social media world? If you find a particular person's page or account triggers you, then exert your power by unfollowing them.

Comparison can feel uncomfortable, but it can also shed light on opportunities for personal growth. Try asking yourself:

- What is it about this that makes me feel incomplete?
- What's this telling me about myself?
- Is this response helpful to my self-esteem? What is a more positive way to look at this?

INCREASE YOUR SELF-WORTH: When we feel good on the inside, we feel less of a need to compare ourselves and gain validation from others. If you feel your self-worth could do with a boost, try reading positive affirmations to yourself in the mirror each day.

AFFIRMATIONS YOU MIGHT CHOOSE TO INCLUDE ARE: "I am enough," "I am worthy of happiness," "I am where I need to be," and "happiness flows toward me with ease."

DIRECTING YOUR THOUGHT TRAIN
TAKING CONTROL OF YOUR INNER CRITIC

"I discovered that when I believed my thoughts,
I suffered, but that when I didn't believe them,
I didn't suffer, and that this is true for every
human being. Freedom is as simple as that."

—*Byron Katie*

We've all climbed onboard our runaway thought train headed toward self-criticism, self-doubt, fear, inadequacy, and anxiety. As our train of thought rides through the dark tunnels of our mind, racing out of control, we can feel like a helpless passenger, trapped on an unwanted trip. But it doesn't have to be this way.

When we cultivate the awareness to view ourselves as the controller of our thought train and not its passenger, we realize we can choose to redirect our thoughts when they go off track. Of course, separating ourselves from the voice and thoughts in our head takes practice and patience.

YOU ARE NOT THE VOICE IN YOUR HEAD

Your inner narrator, the voice that provides a running commentary on your life, whispers worries, and dishes out self-criticism, is not you. You are the observer of your voice and are distinctly different from it. There is a distance between you and your voice that enables you to separate the two and take better control. One of the most effective ways to achieve this is by integrating mindfulness practices into your daily routine.

The goal of mindfulness is not to silence the mind but to cultivate your role as the observer. As you observe your thoughts, you gradually create distance between you and your voice, enabling you to notice passing thoughts without judgment or engagement. Assuming the role of the observer allows us to stop an unhelpful thought in its tracks before it arrives at self-criticism or self-doubt.

Daily Delights

You can try practicing this now by noticing the thoughts that come into your head. As thoughts drift into your consciousness, rather than engage them in a conversation, label the thoughts as thinking or feeling.

For example, if your initial thought is "I feel silly doing this," you would label it as feeling. Or if it's "I wonder if I am doing this right," you would label it as thinking.

Try setting a timer on your phone for one minute to complete this short exercise. Notice as you label your thoughts how you begin to see that you are the observer of the voice and that the voice in your head is not you. You can also take time to notice how labeling helps stop the thought in its tracks and prevent it from going any further.

INNER VOICE AND HAPPINESS

The relationship we have with our inner voice is complex and often secretive. Inside, our voice may be criticizing us or fueling thoughts of anxiety, but outside, we can easily conceal its tortuous tone with a fake smile and laugh. Our inner world, made up of our thoughts and feelings, may not be visible to others, but it's a place where we spend most of our time. And if we want to make it a happier place to live in, then we need to ensure we gain better control of the inhabitants we share it with, especially our inner voice.

Studies have shown that our relationship with our inner voice can serve to increase or decrease our happiness levels. Having a more self-compassionate voice can help improve our psychological well-being.[56] According to research, a critical inner voice can reduce motivation and productivity while increasing symptoms of depression.[57]

Our inner world, made up of our thoughts and feelings, may not be visible to others, but it's a place where we spend most of our time.

Understanding our ability to choose more empowering words and reaching for more useful thoughts can put us back in control and help us build a happier inner world in which we are content to spend our time.

EXERCISE

Developing a Compassionate Inner Voice

We are capable of controlling, redirecting, and changing how our inner voice conveys our thoughts. Here are three tips to help you gain better control over your inner voice.

1. **MINDFULNESS:** Practicing mindfulness can help you exert greater control over your thoughts. If you are new to mindfulness, try experimenting with apps such as Calm or Insight Timer.

2. **BE YOUR OWN BEST FRIEND:** When you feel self-critical, talk to yourself as you would a best friend. Encourage yourself and remind yourself that you are doing the best you can.

3. **USE "I AM" PHRASES:** Using "I am" is a quick and powerful way to reach for more useful and empowering thoughts. I love using these before I give a speech ("I am confident") or at the gym ("I am healthy"). The use of "I am" is a quick and easy way to change where our energy and attention are flowing.

BOUNDARIES THAT WILL MAKE LIFE BOUNDLESS

"You have to be able to set boundaries,
otherwise the rest of the world is telling you
who you are and what you should be doing.
You can still be a nice person and set boundaries."

—Oprah Winfrey

---

magine your daily energy as an invisible bucket of water that you carry in your hands. On some mornings, you wake up to a full bucket, and on other mornings, there's barely enough to fill a cup. As you and your invisible bucket journey through the day, you meet people and engage in activities that either take water out of the bucket or fill it back up.

This energy exchange between people and activities, that can either diminish or renew our energy, requires careful management. Setting boundaries is an essential part of keeping your bucket as full as possible so you can use your energy to work toward what matters most to you.

For some readers, saying no may come easily. For others, the thought of uttering the simple word, "No" can evoke feelings of anxiety and guilt.

I'm certainly no stranger to the flood of people–pleasing panic when someone asks me to do something that I don't want or feel able to do. I've said yes when I meant no far too frequently out of fear that saying no would anger someone or lower their opinion of me.

However, I've come to understand that saying no when your intentions are good can be a loving and compassionate act toward yourself and others. It began with considering if anyone really benefitted from my need to please. Was it really enjoyable for the other person to watch a movie, eat a meal, or work on that project with someone who didn't want to be there? Was it really nice to feel frustrated and resentful because you were always there for others?

As author and researcher Brené Brown says, "Clear is kind. Unclear is unkind." Saying yes when we mean no is unclear and unkind not only to ourselves but to other people who will quickly drain our energy bucket.

SCIENCE *of* BLISS

Research from the University of California in San Francisco shows that people who have greater difficulty saying no increase their likelihood of experiencing burnout, stress, and depression. By learning how to say no and set healthy boundaries, we can minimize our experience of negative emotions and cultivate happiness.[58]

Being clear on our boundaries and being honest with ourselves and others about how we feel is an act of authenticity and love. It's through saying no that we create space for the other person to find someone who wants to participate in what's being asked of them. This also allows us to protect our energy and time, ensuring that we invest in what matters most in our lives. Sometimes this can mean we have to establish significantly uncomfortable boundaries in friendships, families, relationships, and work.

If you're in the process of constructing those firm boundaries, I appreciate that it can be a stressful and emotional whirlwind. Just remember, although sometimes it's helpful to gain the opinion of others, trust your gut and follow your inner intuition. After all, these are your boundaries, and often there is no right answer, just the answer that feels right for you right now.

happy TIP

When saying no, use "I don't" instead of "I can't." Research shows that the use of "I can't" implies they are resisting temptation and their decision could be up for debate, compared with people that used "I don't." So instead of saying "I can't do after work drinks during the week," say "I don't drink during the week."[59]

E X E R C I S E

Mastering Saying No

Saying no can be a challenging but essential skill. Here are my top three tips to help master the art of no.

1. PREPARE A PHRASE: When you are asked to do something that you don't want to or aren't able to commit to, it's easy to panic and say yes. However, having a phrase already prepared can help. For example, you can say "I think it's a going to be a no for now, but I'll let you know if anything changes," or "Thanks for asking but I can't (insert the ask). I hope you find someone who can (insert the ask)."

2. PROTECT YOUR TIME: It's hard to say no when you haven't intentionally blocked out how you want to use your time. By clearly planning when you're going to exercise, work, and catch up with friends, it makes it harder for other people's priorities to nudge their way into your calendar.

3. VALUE YOUR INTEGRITY: If you don't want to go out to dinner or volunteer for that extra project at work, it's OK to say no. After all, it's better to say no and be yourself than to say yes and pretend to be someone you aren't.

THE CURIOSITY CURE

> "Curiosity only does one thing, and that is to give.
> And what it gives you are clues on
> the incredible scavenger hunt of your life."
>
> —*Elizabeth Gilbert*

Overthinking poses a real threat to our ability to be in the present moment. As our minds sink into obsessing over what we should or shouldn't do, they send our thoughts dashing between the future and the past looking for answers. This creates a messy, tangled web of thought, and along with the heavy self-inflicted pressure for us to "make the right choice" or "do the right thing," it consumes our attention.

As a result, we struggle to focus on the present moment as our minds tend to obsess about finding the perfect answer. While it's wise to give deep thought to our decisions, we should also be mindful not to mislead ourselves to believe that life is a problem that can be solved solely in our heads. After all, even our most intricately woven plans and carefully thought through intentions can come undone in the tangled tapestry of life.

Overthinking our decisions can leave us standing on the sidelines of life. Our fear of making the wrong decision can lead us to over-analyze and over-invite other people's opinions into the process. Too much information can overwhelm us, leading to decision fatigue and procrastination. It can feel more comfortable to give up before we've even started.

Curiosity, on the other hand, playfully nudges us forward, urging us to experiment. It whispers, "I wonder how it would feel if you did that?"

Curiosity is different from being impulsive. Curiosity doesn't dive right in to the deep end. Instead, it dips a toe in the water, sees how it feels, then makes an informed decision about what to do next. Its slow, steady, and experimental approach opens up new perspectives, broadens our horizons, and replaces the heavy burden of "getting it right" with "I'm just curious to see what happens." When we choose curiosity, we open ourselves up to the present moment and nurture a more profound connection with our own intuition and the wider world.

> *Curiosity doesn't dive right in to the deep end.*

Curiosity can ignite a love affair with life, and studies have found that people who cultivate curiosity have a higher level of life satisfaction.[60] When we are in a state of curiosity, our brains can retain more information,[61] generate alternatives, and boost our creativity—all vital and helpful qualities for making choices.[62]

Furthermore, curiosity connects us to valuable feedback on how we feel about the action we're taking, which enables us to experiment more with life. Curiosity's playful approach can help erode our fear of failure and teach us how to fully engage in the feeling of what it means to be alive. Psychologists have demonstrated that people who are more curious have more meaningful lives, suggesting that curiosity is a choice that moves us toward a deeper sense of purpose.[63]

Daily Delights

When we feel trapped in overthinking, it can be helpful to remind ourselves that life is not a test or a box-tick exercise. Instead, it's one big exciting (and at times scary) experiment in which you co-create your reality with the unpredictable external world. The best lab partner you could have to assist you in this experiment is curiosity.

EXERCISE

Cultivating Curiosity

Try applying these three simple steps to cultivate more curiosity in your life.

1. ASK QUESTIONS: Curiosity questions help us generate possibilities, creative solutions, and ideas. If you feel weighed down by a decision in the present moment, try sparking your curiosity by asking:

- What if...?

- I wonder what would happen if...?

- How might I...?

- If anything was possible right now, what would I do?

- If I couldn't fail, what action would I take?

- What small step could I take that would give me feedback on how I feel about this?

2. LISTEN TO FEEDBACK: Asking questions of yourself or others is a powerful way to feed your curiosity, but only if you listen to the feedback. If you're curious about learning how someone achieved a goal you want, listen to their answers. Notice the patterns or common themes that emerge and listen to your own inner guidance.

3. ACT: Taking action is critical for curiosity. Try different approaches, take small steps every day toward what matters most, and curiosity will scatter a breadcrumb trail toward ideas, opportunities, people, and your passions.

INVEST IN CONNECTION

"To love at all is to be vulnerable."

—*C. S. Lewis*

Happiness is letting go of who we think we should be and being seen for who we are. This is challenging when we live in a society where the question following "what's your name?" is "what do you do for a living?"

We grow up learning to show people all our shiny, surface-level accomplishments and conceal the beautiful, messy patterns that lie beneath. But it's exhausting when relationships feel more like job interviews than real connections. Our resistance and apprehension to be ourselves prevents us from cultivating deep, meaningful, human connections. Research suggests that a lack of connection can make us unhappy.

Taking time to develop meaningful relationships in the present can offer a sanctuary for us to drop the mask, laugh, share, cry, and grow without feeling judged. What's more, making this investment is likely to give us high returns on our happiness and health.

There's a paradox emerging in our technological world: we're both more connected and more disconnected than ever.

According to a recent survey, more than three in five Americans are lonely, with a rising number reporting that they felt left out and misunderstood. The survey also revealed a sobering relationship between social media and loneliness, finding that seventy-three percent of very heavy social media users considered themselves lonely, compared with fifty-two percent of light users.

The study also found that eighteen to twenty-two year-olds had the highest average loneliness score. Psychologist Julianne Holt-Lunstad, a professor at Brigham Young University, urges us to recognize that when it comes to feeling isolated, "No one is immune."[64]

That said, the research points to connection as the remedy to heal our loneliness and ease the pain of feeling misunderstood. Connection nourishes both the body and the mind, and studies show that people who have strong ties live longer, have fewer health issues, and are generally happier.[65]

SCIENCE *of* BLISS

Perhaps the most compelling evidence for making this investment comes from the world's longest study on happiness, conducted by Harvard. The study that spanned almost eighty years concluded that, "Close relationships, more than money or fame, are what keep people happy throughout their lives."[66]

AUTHENTIC CONNECTION AND HAPPINESS

Part of choosing to be happy in the present is choosing to cultivate genuine, vulnerable relationships where we feel safe to drop the mask, share our mess, and speak our truth. There is an extensive body of research that shows that investing in our connections really pays off.

While sharing the messy moments, irrational thoughts, and embarrassing moments in life can feel daunting, a study by researchers at the University of Mannheim found that it's actually a quality we admire in others. The researchers wrote that "showing vulnerability might sometimes feel more like weakness from the inside...[but] to others, these acts might look more like courage from the outside."[67]

Through cultivating authentic connection, we have the strength to be vulnerable. We set ourselves free from the expectation that life should be perfect and embrace our humanity for the beautiful mess it is.

EXERCISE

Growing Your Connections

We'll all be on different scales of the connection spectrum, and our circumstances will be unique. However, to start the process, read the points below to grow your connections at the stage most relevant to you.

PLANT: Making new connections as an adult can be a challenge, but we can take small steps to plant the seeds of friendship. A good starting point is to use sites like Meetup.com or go to local classes, gyms, or clubs to connect with like-minded groups of people.

Remember to tune in to how you feel around a new person. Pay attention to whether it feels natural, whether you feel like you can be yourself, and how you feel after spending time with the person.

NURTURE: It's easy for our busy lives to take over and have us paying less attention to the existing friendships we have. Think about how you could nurture existing friendships more. It can be useful to make meeting up a ritual, perhaps a payday dinner date each month or movie Mondays. Creating rituals can take the hassle out of comparing diaries and develops a close bond through a shared experience.

GROW: Strong connections can offer a safe place for us to share and grow. It can be useful to think about how you could encourage a bit more vulnerability with your friends. Also, notice if you are facing some similar challenges and reflect on how you might be able to grow together.

Play allows all of our whirling impulses and worries to dissolve. Our sense of self disappears, and we melt into unity with the present moment. Use play as a blissful retreat from the game of life and a return to childlike wonder.

5 ways
TO SAVOR THE PRESENT

1. PRACTICE GRATITUDE

Our disappointment in the present moment is often caused when our expectations don't match reality. Practicing gratitude can help ground us and stop our thoughts from snowballing out of control.

It's easy to scoff at gratitude for being overly simplistic, but it's hard to argue with the wealth of research that's demonstrated its effectiveness. Look around you, notice the obvious things to be grateful for, then turn your attention to more obscure fortunes.

2. GET OUT AND INTO NATURE

Research has found that spending 120 minutes per week in nature improves our health and well-being.[68] Consider how you could take more time to be in nature. If you live in a city, contemplate how you could integrate nature into your home with plants or window boxes to give the soothing effects it offers.

3. EXERCISE

According to research, even a little exercise (just ten minutes) is enough to lift and improve our mood. Better yet, the study also showed that the type of activity doesn't matter, so whether you walk, squat, or stretch out with some yoga moves, the choice is yours.[69]

4. PERFORM A SMALL ACT OF KINDNESS

Kindness is a virtuous cycle that makes us and other people feel good. Small acts of kindness are a reminder to us and others that we are part of something greater than ourselves. Research has also shown that when we act out of generosity, our well-being and self-esteem improve. Even small acts, like lifting something someone has dropped, can boost our happiness.[70]

5. DO ANYTHING, BUT NOT EVERYTHING

If you can bring anything to the present moment, let it be intention. We live in a world where business is a badge of honor and overscheduling is commonplace. Grant yourself permission to slow down. Time is our most precious resource, and considering how we want to spend it is inextricably linked to a life well lived.

"Very little is needed to make a happy life; it is all within yourself."

—*Marcus Aurelius*

CHOOSE HAPPY, CHOOSE WISELY

Happiness is what drives us. We wouldn't want to be successful if we didn't think it would make us happy. But increasingly, I wonder if we've been channeling our energies in the wrong direction.

We live on a finite planet with finite resources and yet we are promised an infinite amount of happiness. We're led to believe we can have everything we ever wanted as long as we pursue it. If we work hard enough, happiness will be ours.

This endless purist feeds our busy culture, causes us to constantly consume, puts our planet under strain, and somehow leaves us always starving for more.

Choice tries to tell us something different.

Choosing happiness isn't about snap decisions or judgements. It's pausing in the present, considering our options, and moving forward to the best of our current abilities. Choice, when used wisely, asks us to consider our individual and collective needs. And because choice takes the blinkers off and lets us exit the happiness race, it will help us consider how we can raise each other up rather than keep each other down.

We won't always make the right choices, and some of us will be more constrained by our choices than others. But choice does give us the peace of mind that we did our best with the knowledge and circumstances we faced at that time.

So as our present becomes our past and our past becomes our future, we move through life reassured that we made the best choices we could have with the information we had. That can only make for a life well lived. A happy life.

BIBLIOGRAPHY

1. Brickman, P., Coates, D., & Janoff-Bulman, R. (1978). Lottery winners and accident victims: Is happiness relative?. Journal of personality and social psychology, 36(8), 917.

2. Niemiec, Christopher P., Richard M. Ryan, and Edward L. Deci. (June 2009) "The path taken: Consequences of Attaining Intrinsic and Extrinsic Aspirations in Post-College Life." J Res Pers.

3. Newman, K. M. (2014, December 22). Variety is the Spice of Emotional Life. Greater Good Science Centre. https://greatergood.berkeley.edu/article/item/variety_is_the_spice_of_emotional_life

4. Diener, E., & Tay, L. (2017). A scientific review of the remarkable benefits of happiness for successful and healthy living. Happiness, 90.

5. *Society for Personality and Social Psychology. (August 8 2014)* How we form habits, change existing ones. ScienceDaily. Retrieved December 3, 2019 retrieved via www.sciencedaily.com/releases/2014/08/140808111931.htm

6. Wood, W., & Rünger, D. (2016). *Psychology of habit.* Annual review of psychology, 67.

7. Clear, J (2018). *Atomic Habits. An Easy & Proven Way To Build Good Habits and Break Bad Ones.* Avery. Penguin Random House LLC. New York. Page 15

8 & 9. Gardner, B., Lally, P., & Wardle, J. (2012). *Making health habitual: the psychology of 'habit-formation' and general practice.* The British journal of general practice : the journal of the Royal College of General Practitioners, 62(605), 664–666. https://doi.org/10.3399/bjgp12X659466

10. Blair R. (2012). Considering anger from a cognitive neuroscience perspective. Wiley interdisciplinary reviews. Cognitive science, 3(1), 65–74. https://doi.org/10.1002/wcs.154

11. Devlin, H (2019 May, 12). *Science of Anger: how gender, age, and personality shape this emotion.* The *Guardian.* Retrieved from via https://www.theguardian.com/lifeandstyle/2019/may/12/science-of-anger-gender-age-personality

12. Universidad Complutense de Madrid. (2016, June 15). First direct evidence for ultra-fast responses in the human amygdala to fear. ScienceDaily. Retrieved December 2, 2019, from www.sciencedaily.com/releases/2016/06/160615095132.htm

13. Hamilton, D (Dec 2015) *Calming Your Brain During Conflict.* Harvard Business Review. Retrieved online via https://hbr.org/2015/12/calming-your-brain-during-conflict

14. Bushman, B. J. (2002). *Does venting anger feed or extinguish the flame? Catharsis, rumination, distraction, anger and aggressive responding.* Personality and Social Psychology Bulletin, 28(6), 724–731. https://doi.org/10.1177/0146167202289002

15. Fitzgibbons, R. P. (1986). The cognitive and emotive uses of forgiveness in the treatment of anger. Psychotherapy: Theory, Research, Practice, Training, 23(4), 629.

16. Hillman, J. (1996). *The soul's code: In search of character and calling.* New York: Random House.

17. Jung, C. G. (1933). *Modern man in search of a soul. Pg. 111* Harcourt, Brace.

18. Albarracín, D., & Wyer, R. S., Jr (2000). *The cognitive impact of past behavior: influences on beliefs, attitudes, and future behavioral decisions.* Journal of personality and social psychology, 79(1), 5–22. doi:10.1037//0022-3514.79.1.5

19. A. Jha. (2005, June 30) "Where belief is born"The Guardian Retrieved from https://www.theguardian.com/science/2005/jun/30/psychology.neuroscience

20. Wong, K (2017, December 28) "Why Self Compassion Beats Self Confidence," New York Times retrived from https://www.nytimes.com/2017/12/28/smarter-living/why-self-compassion-beats-self-confidence.html

21. Heslin, P. A. (1999). *Boosting Empowerment by Developing Self-efficacy.* Asia Pacific Journal of Human Resources, 37(1), 52–64. https://doi.org/10.1177/103841119903700105

22. Frey, W. H., 2nd, DeSota-Johnson, D., Hoffman, C., & McCall, J. T. (1981). *Effect of stimulus on the chemical composition of human tears.* American journal of ophthalmology, 92(4), 559–567. https://doi.org/10.1016/0002-9394(81)90651-6

23. Maltby, John & Day, Liza & Barber, Louise. (2005). *Forgiveness and happiness. The differing contexts of forgiveness using the distinction between hedonic and eudaimonic happiness.* Journal of Happiness Studies. 6. 1-13. 10.1007/s10902-004-0924-9.

24. Tamir, Maya. (2017, August 14). *Secret to Happiness May Include More Unpleasant Emotions.* The American Psychological Association. https://www.apa.org/news/press/releases/2017/08/secret-happiness

25. Kacewicz, E., Slatcher, R. B., & Pennebaker, J. W. (2007). *Expressive writing: An alternative to traditional methods.* In *Low-cost approaches to promote physical and mental health* (pp. 271-284). Springer, New York, NY.

26. American Psychological Association (2019, October) "The Great Unknown: 10 tips for dealing with the stress of uncertainity," https://www.apa.org/helpcenter/stress-uncertainty

27. Bar-Anan, Y., Wilson, T. D., & Gilbert, D. T. (2009). *The feeling of uncertainty intensifies affective reactions.* Emotion, 9(1), 123.

28. Brooks, A. C (2017, October 21) "Fear Can Make You a Better Person," The Atlantic, retrived via https://www.theatlantic.com/science/archive/2017/10/how-fear-can-make-you-a-better-person/544454/

29. Murphy, K (2017, October 26) "Outsmarting Our Primitive Responses to Fear" The New York Times retrived via https://www.nytimes.com/2017/10/26/well/live/fear-anxiety-therapy.html

30. Kircanski, K., Lieberman, M. D., & Craske, M. G. (2012). *Feelings into words: contributions of language to exposure therapy.* Psychological science, 23(10), 1086-1091

31. Bryson, B (2019) *The Body: A Guide for Occupants,* Doubleday

32. Summer Allen, P (2018, September 26) "Eight Reasons Why Awe Makes Your Life Better," Greater Good Science Centre , retrived from https://greatergood.berkeley.edu/article/item/eight_reasons_why_awe_makes_your_life_better

33. Rudd, M., Vohs, K. D., & Aaker, J. (2012). *Awe expands people's perception of time, alters decision making, and enhances well-being.* Psychological science, 23(10), 1130-1136.

34. van Elk, M., Arciniegas Gomez, M. A., van der Zwaag, W., van Schie, H. T., & Sauter, D. (2019). *The neural correlates of the awe experience: Reduced default mode network activity during feelings of awe.* Human brain mapping, 40(12), 3561-3574.

35. Piff, P. K., Dietze, P., Feinberg, M., Stancato, D. M., & Keltner, D. (2015). *Awe, the small self, and prosocial behavior.* Journal of personality and social psychology, 108(6), 883.

36. Chirico, A., Cipresso, P., Yaden, D. B., Biassoni, F., Riva, G., & Gaggioli, A. (2017). *Effectiveness of immersive videos in inducing awe: an experimental study.* Scientific Reports, 7(1), 1-11.

37. Bonebright, C. A., Clay, D. L., & Ankenmann, R. D. (2000). *The relationship of workaholism with work–life conflict, life satisfaction, and purpose in life.* Journal of counseling psychology, 47(4), 469.

38. Association for Psychological Science (2016, November 6) "Sense of meaning and purpose linked to longer lifespan" Science Daily, retrieved via https://www.sciencedaily.com/releases/2014/11/141106211618.htm

39. Dolan, E. W (2020, January 6) "New psychology study indicates pursuing evolutionary-relevant goals provides purpose in life" Retrived via https://www.psypost.org/2020/01/new-psychology-study-indicates-pursuing-evolutionary-relevant-goals-provides-purpose-in-life-55163

40. Anxiety and Depression Association of America, "Facts and Statistics" retrived from https://adaa.org/about-adaa/press-room/facts-statistics

41. Deng, J., Li, T., Wang, J., & Zhang, R. (2020). *Optimistically accepting suffering boosts happiness: Associations between Buddhism patience, selflessness, and subjective authentic-durable happiness.* Journal of Happiness Studies, 21(1), 223-240

42 & 43. Schnitker, S. A. (2012). An examination of patience and well-being. The Journal of Positive Psychology, 7(4), 263-280

44. Crocker, J., & Knight, K. M. (2005). *Contingencies of self-worth. Current directions in psychological science,* 14(4), 200-203.

45. Neff, K. D., Kirkpatrick, K. L., & Rude, S. S. (2007). *Self-compassion and adaptive psychological functioning.* Journal of research in personality, 41(1), 139-154.

46. Bradt, S (2010, November 11) "Wandering mind not a happy mind," The Harvard Gazette, https://news.harvard.edu/gazette/story/2010/11/wandering-mind-not-a-happy-mind/

47. McLean, K. C., & Pasupathi, M. (2011). *Narrative Identity*. Encyclopedia of Adolescence 1846-1849.

48. Bauer, J. J., McAdams, D. P., & Pals, J. L. (2008). *Narrative identity and eudaimonic well-being.* Journal of happiness studies, 9(1), 81-104

49. McLean, K. C., & Pratt, M. W. (2006). *Life's little (and big) lessons: Identity statuses and meaning-making in the turning point narratives of emerging adults.* Developmental psychology, 42(4), 714.

50. Adler, J. M., Turner, A. F., Brookshier, K. M., Monahan, C., Walder-Biesanz, I., Harmeling, L. H., ... Oltmanns, T. F. (2015). *Variation in narrative identity is associated with trajectories of mental health over several years.* Journal of personality and social psychology, 108(3), 476–496. doi:10.1037/a0038601

51. Proyer, R. T. (2013). *The well-being of playful adults: Adult playfulness, subjective well-being, physical well-being, and the pursuit of enjoyable activities.* The European Journal of Humour Research, 1(1), 84-98.

52. Adams, G. S., & Inesi, M. E. (2016). *Impediments to forgiveness: Victim and transgressor attributions of intent and guilt.* Journal of Personality and Social Psychology, 111(6), 866–881. https://doi.org/10.1037/pspi0000070

53. Fowler, J. H., & Christakis, N. A. (2008). *Dynamic spread of happiness in a large social network: longitudinal analysis over 20 years in the Framingham Heart Study.* BMJ (Clinical research ed.), 337, a2338. https://doi.org/10.1136/bmj.a2338

54. White, J. B., Langer, E. J., Yariv, L., & Welch, J. C. (2006). *Frequent social comparisons and destructive emotions and behaviors: The dark side of social comparisons.* Journal of adult development, 13(1), 36-44.

55. Lup, K., Trub, L., & Rosenthal, L. (2015). *Instagram# instasad?: exploring associations among instagram use, depressive symptoms, negative social comparison, and strangers followed.* Cyberpsychology, Behavior, and Social Networking, 18(5), 247-252.

56. Zessin, U., Dickhäuser, O., & Garbade, S. (2015). *The Relationship Between Self-Compassion and Well-Being: A Meta-Analysis. Applied psychology.* Health and well-being, 7(3), 340–364. https://doi.org/10.1111/aphw.12051

57. Kannan, D., & Levitt, H. M. (2013). *A review of client self-criticism in psychotherapy.* Journal of Psychotherapy Integration, 23(2), 166–178. https://doi.org/10.1037/a0032355

58. Bradberry, T (2013, March 11) "The Art of Saying No," Forbes, Retrieved from https://www.forbes.com/sites/travisbradberry/2013/03/11/the-art-of-saying-no/#670474ea4ca8

59. Patrick, V. M., & Hagtvedt, H. (2012). "I don't" versus "I can't": When empowered refusal motivates goal-directed behavior. Journal of Consumer Research, 39(2), 371-381

60. Peterson, C., Ruch, W., Beermann, U., Park, N., & Seligman, M. E. (2007). *Strengths of character, orientations to happiness, and life satisfaction.* The journal of positive psychology, 2(3), 149-156.

61. Gruber, M. J., Gelman, B. D., & Ranganath, C. (2014). *States of curiosity modulate hippocampus-dependent learning via the dopaminergic circuit.* Neuron, 84(2), 486-496.

62. Gino, F (2018, September-October Issue) "The Business Case for Curiosity," Harvard Business Review, retrived from https://hbr.org/2018/09/curiosity

63. Kashdan, T. B., & Steger, M. F. (2007). *Curiosity and pathways to well-being and meaning in life: Traits, states, and everyday behaviors.* Motivation and Emotion, 31(3), 159-173.

64. Renken, E (2020, January 23) "Most Americans Are Lonely, And Our Workplace Culture May Not Be Helping," NPR 23 retrived via https://www.npr.org/sections/health-shots/2020/01/23/798676465/most-americans-are-lonely-and-our-workplace-culture-may-not-be-helping?t=1582644209644.&t=1585316026513

65. Watch, H.W.H (2019, August 6) "The health benefits of strong relationships," Harvard Health Publishing Harvard Medical School retrived via https://www.health.harvard.edu/newsletter_article/the-health-benefits-of-strong-relationships

66. Mineo, L (2017, April 11) "Good genes are nice, but joy is better," The Harvard Gazette. Retrieved via https://news.harvard.edu/gazette/story/2017/04/over-nearly-80-years-harvard-study-has-been-showing-how-to-live-a-healthy-and-happy-life/.

67. Newman K M, (2018, November 5) "Why Is It So Hard to Be Vulnerable?," Greater Good Magazine,retived via https://greatergood.berkeley.edu/article/item/why_is_it_so_hard_to_be_vulnerable

68. White, M. P., Alcock, I., Grellier, J., Wheeler, B. W., Hartig, T., Warber, S. L., ... & Fleming, L. E. (2019). *Spending at least 120 minutes a week in nature is associated with good health and wellbeing.* Scientific reports, 9(1), 1-11.

69. Zhang, Z., & Chen, W. (2019). *A systematic review of the relationship between physical activity and happiness.* Journal of happiness studies, 20(4), 1305-1322.

70. Summer Allen, P (2018) "The Science of Generosity," Greater Good Science Centre , vol. White Paper prepared for the John Templeton Foundation.

INDEX

ACKNOWLEDGMENTS

I'm honored to share these beautiful acknowledgements submitted by my readers. Each one made my heart swell and brought a beautiful reminder that happiness lies in our connection to one another.

· My boys, you are beautiful, you are unique, you are loved. Embrace your individuality because you are exactly who you are meant to be. Never stop being curious, never settle for less and always brush your teeth!—Your Mum, Oonagh Tierney

· To my Mum, I am so proud of how you looked for a little drop of happiness in each Dark day. I promised you all the little drops of Happy would one day bring you back to brighter days. You bring so much Happiness to us all. Love Always, Suzie Gates

· My life partner, Steve Wood—10 years in 2021 Merci! For all our laughs and your ridiculous happiness for life as we survive this zombie apocalypse together! Being around you makes everything better. Every day we keep on choosing each other and I love it! Steve—you're gorgeous—Charlotte Pedersen

· My parents Angel & Linda, who have shown me what true, genuine, selfless love looks like between two people. You've been my biggest supporters through every steppingstone in my life no matter how small. You've taught me how to search for God's love and to remember there's always a bigger plan, and for that I'm eternally grateful. With love, your daughter Sarah Pando

I'd like to personally acknowledge my publisher Rage Kindelsperger, words will never describe my depth of gratitude. The opportunities you've provided me with to write have had a profound impact on my life. A heartfelt thank you.

To my editor, Leeann Moreau, thank you for your thoughtful insight, wise guidance, and the careful attention you give to the reader's experience. It's been an absolute joy to work on *Choose Happy* with you.

To Quarto, thank you for making beautiful books that are appealing to read. It is a privilege to have my words infused with the talent from your wonderful art and design team.

I'd like to express my deep gratitude for my friends Janet, Helen, Cathy C, Orlaith & Carly—life's better with you in it.

To Cathy Ryan, for our deep and meaningful chats that started when we were thirteen and have continued since. Every time I see you the world feels brighter and lighter.

To Kylie Turner, for enduring my endless rambles. I treasure sorting through the pieces of life's great jigsaw puzzle with you.

To Nuala Tyrer, we became inseparable friends at school and have been by each other's sides ever since. It's been a joy to see you become the most amazing mother to Norah and Harry. Nothing makes me happier than adventuring through this crazy, amazing world with you as my friend.

ABOUT THE AUTHOR

Sarah is a Northern Irish girl with a huge passion for unlocking human potential (you could call it a bit of an obsession). Sarah is a member of the British Psychological Society, a coach, business coach, and Neuro-Linguistic Programming Practitioner. She's helped hundreds of ambitious individuals and businesses to dream big and take consistent action to get the results, with ease. In 2016 Sarah left her job and went in pursuit of her dream to work and travel full-time. She now runs The Power to Reinvent and helps people across the world fulfill their potential and feel happier. Learn more at www.thepowertoreinvent.com or connect with Sarah on Instagram @thepowertoreinvent